Drawing
Still life

By
Prosenjit & Arundhati

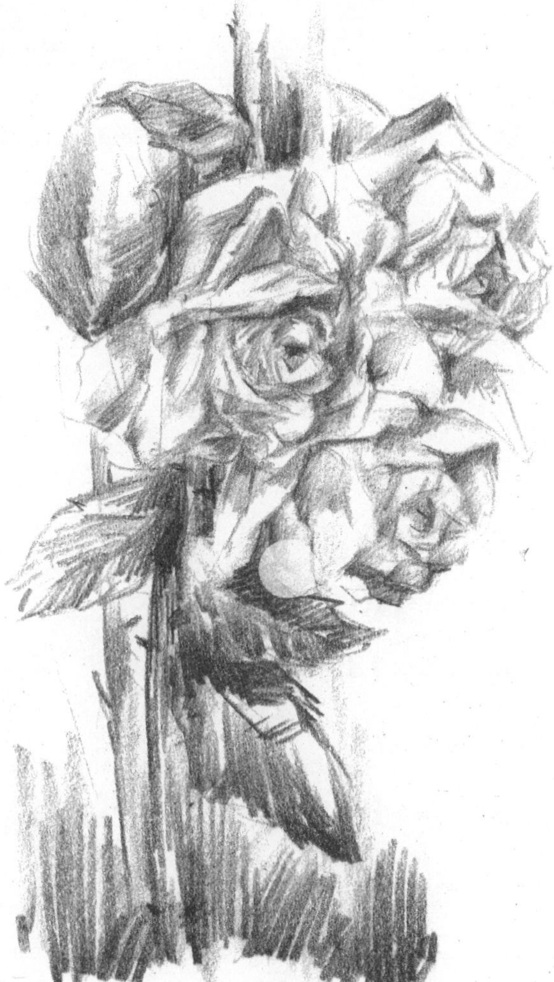

UNICORN BOOKS

ISBN: 978-81-7806-167-2

UNICORN BOOKS Pvt. Ltd.
F-2/16, Ansari Road, Daryaganj, New Delhi-110002
Phones: 011-23262683, 23250704, Fax: 011-23257790
email: info@unicornbooks.in
Website: www.unicornbooks.in

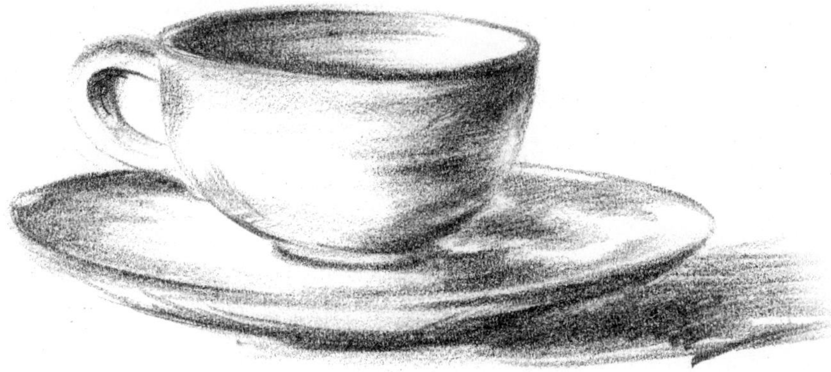

Contents

Introduction

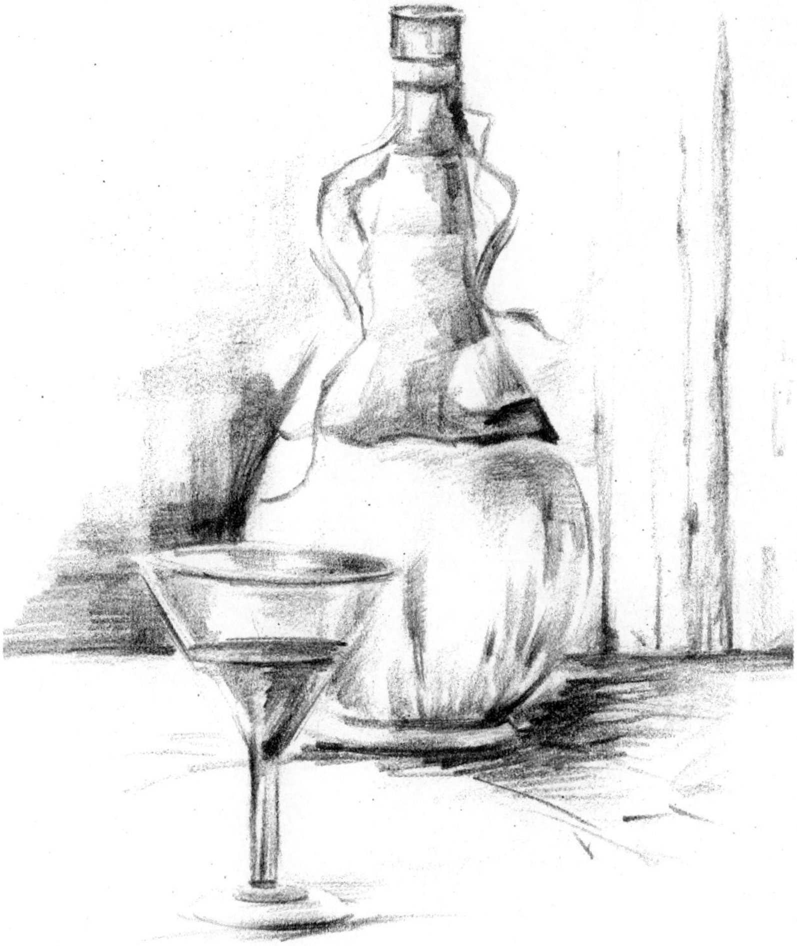

Nature provides almost everything to us. Still life study involves all these elements that we find in nature.

Studying still life involves volume, line drawing, tone drawing, structural drawing, pencil shading and colour. While studying still life we will differentiate between light and shade in the background and the foreground.

To draw still life, keep all the above mentioned points in your mind and go through this book as it will enable you to grasp the basics of still life drawing and other related aspects properly.

We assure you that you will be able to grasp and see a big change in your artistic talents by the time you reach the last page.

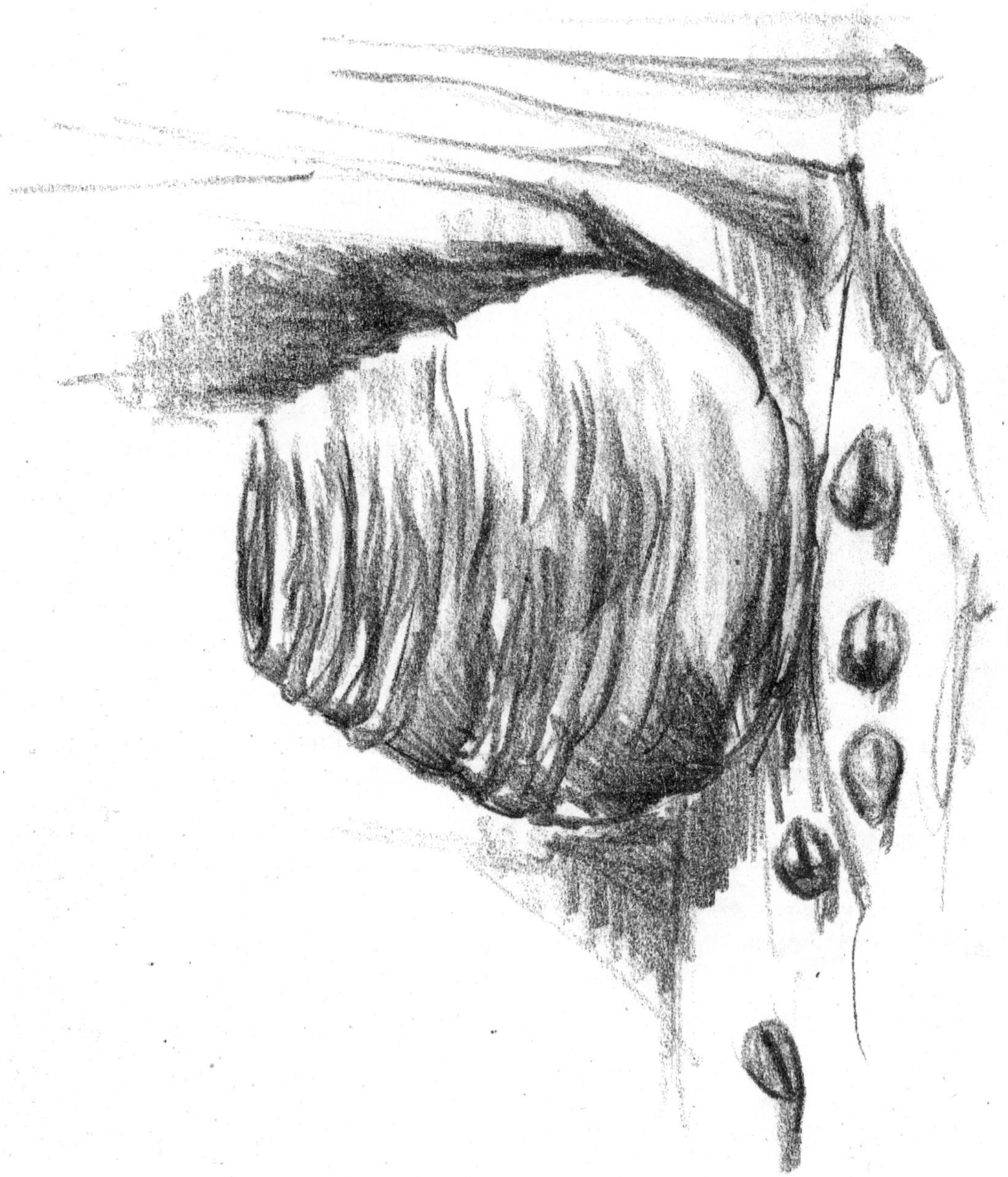

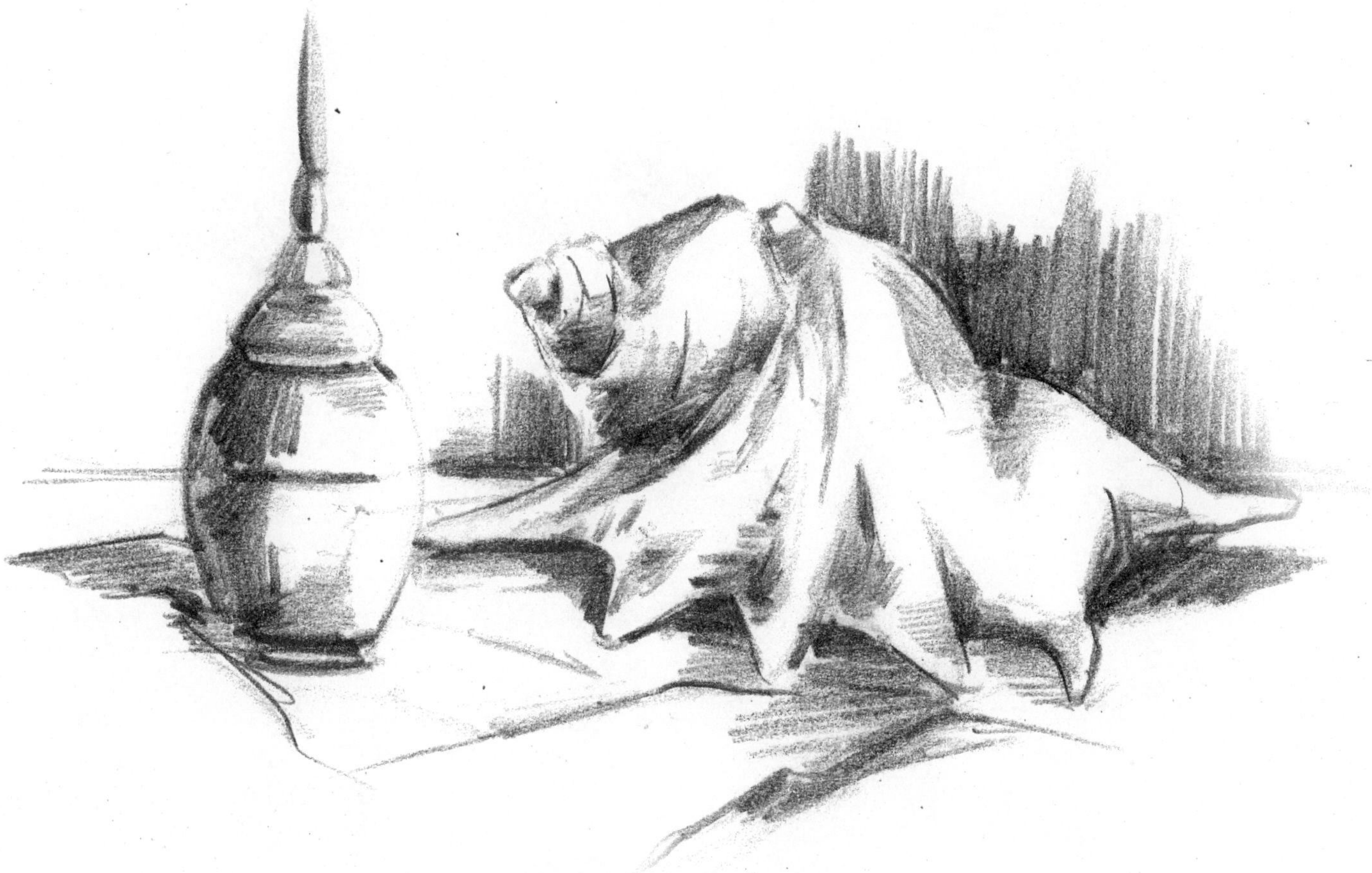

Draw in an easy manner. With time you will become perfect in handing your pencil and in using paper and its texture. White cartridge paper, tinted paper and mount board are some of the working surface I have used in these drawings. Pencil which will give you great results and satisfaction are 2B,4B,6B and black conte crayon. Which one you would like to use to draw a certain thing is up to you.

Pencil stroke plays an important role in drawing. In case of still life drawing, the appropriate usage of pencil makes it able to understand the proper character and texture of the subject.

Still life drawing involves the proper usage of 2B, 4B and 6B strokes of pencil as well as the particular depth of the object. For instance, to get from light to dark shades we need to use 2B, 4B and 6B pencils step by step, where it makes easy to understand the light tone, middle tone and dark tone of the object properly.

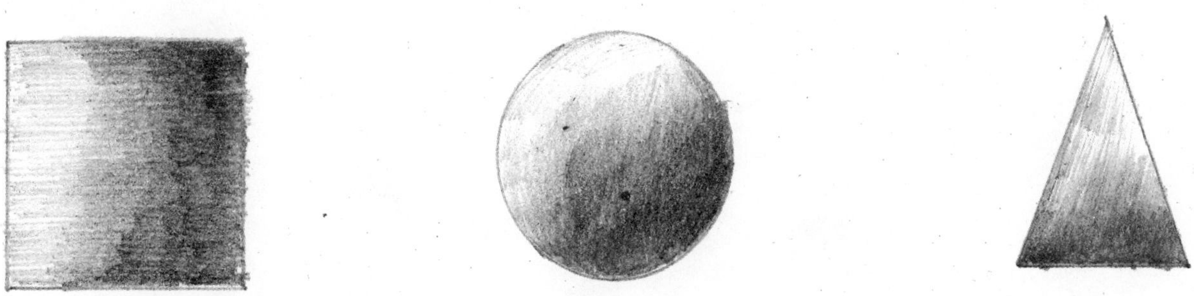

Basic Things of Drawing

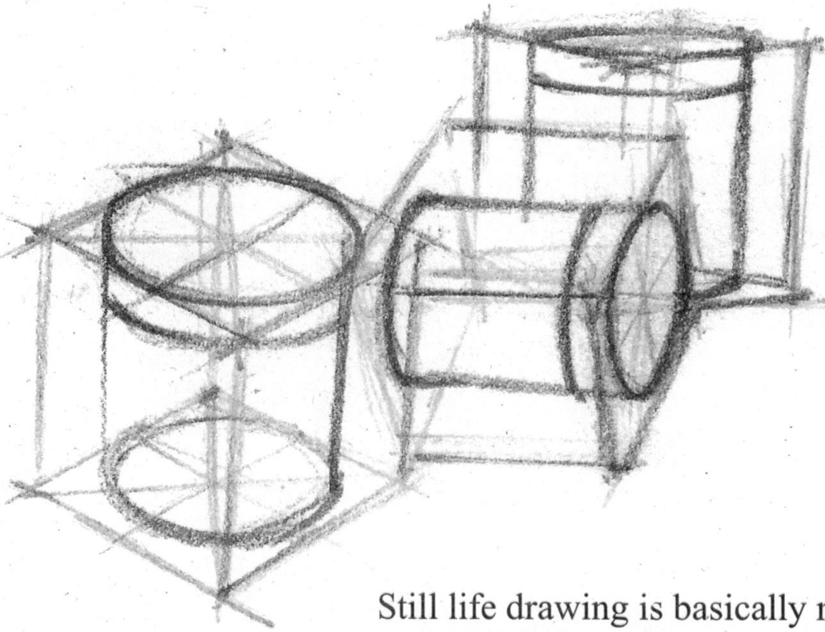

Still life drawing is basically materialistic, so we should have the basic and clear knowledge of object drawing. To draw a particular object we can use its suggestion line to draw an imaginary box. If we use this imaginary box we can get the actual placement of the particular object in the box, which will make it easy to draw it.

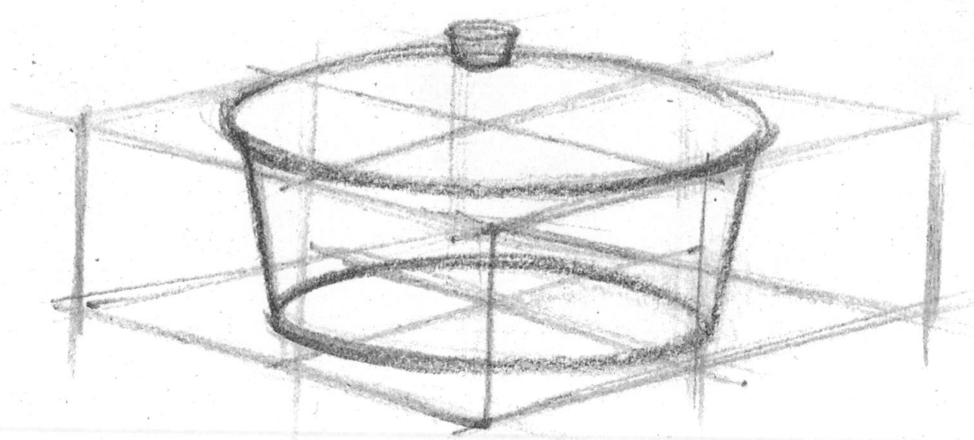

Still life drawing involves many kinds of objects, and to draw them, we need the same usage of the imaginary box and its placement to get the actual subject as well as its composition.

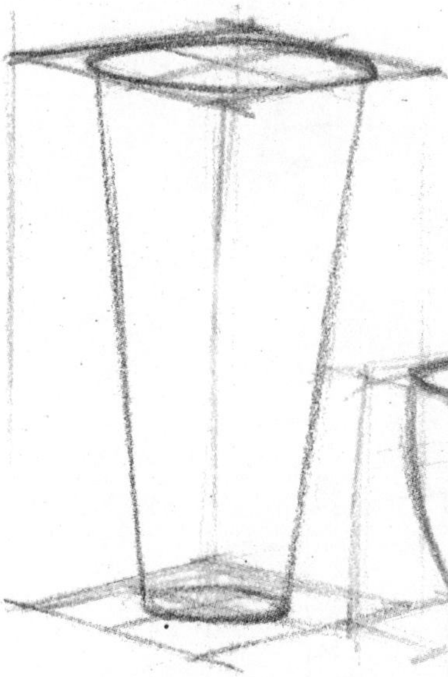

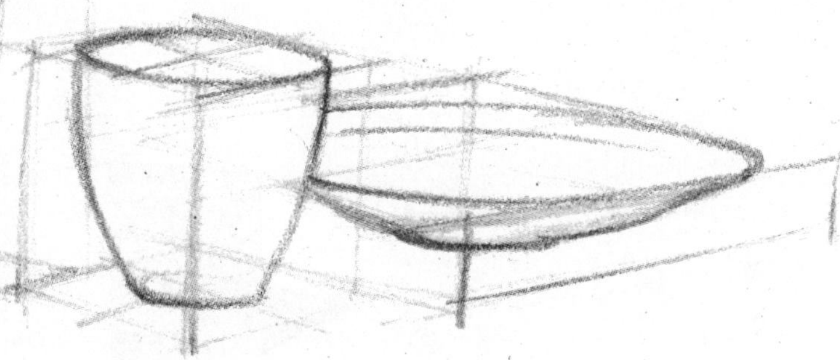

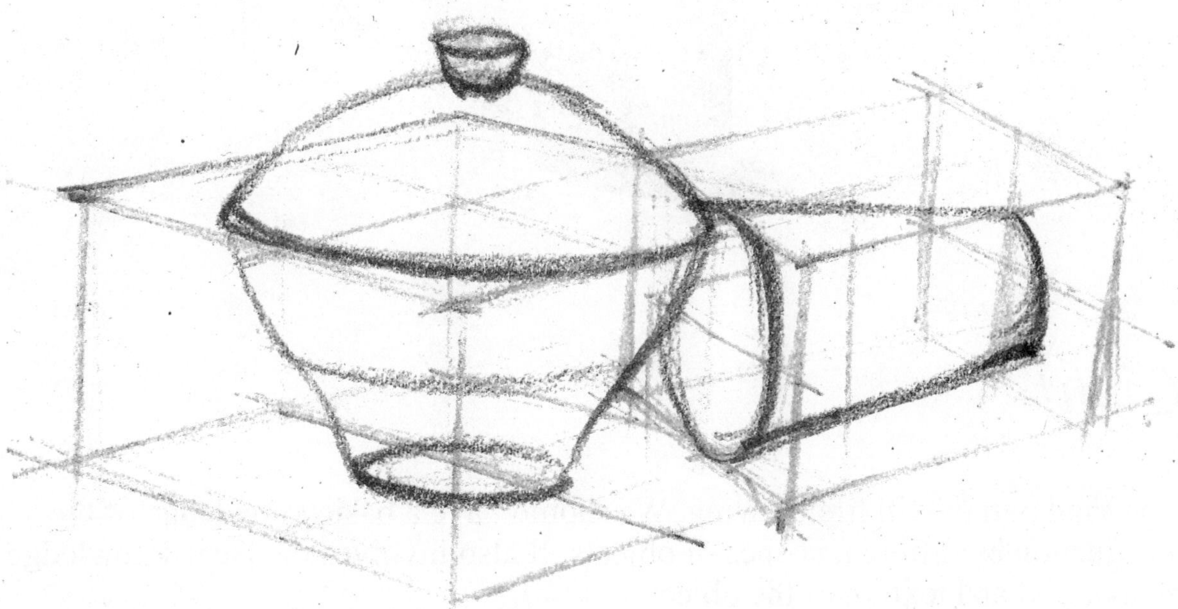

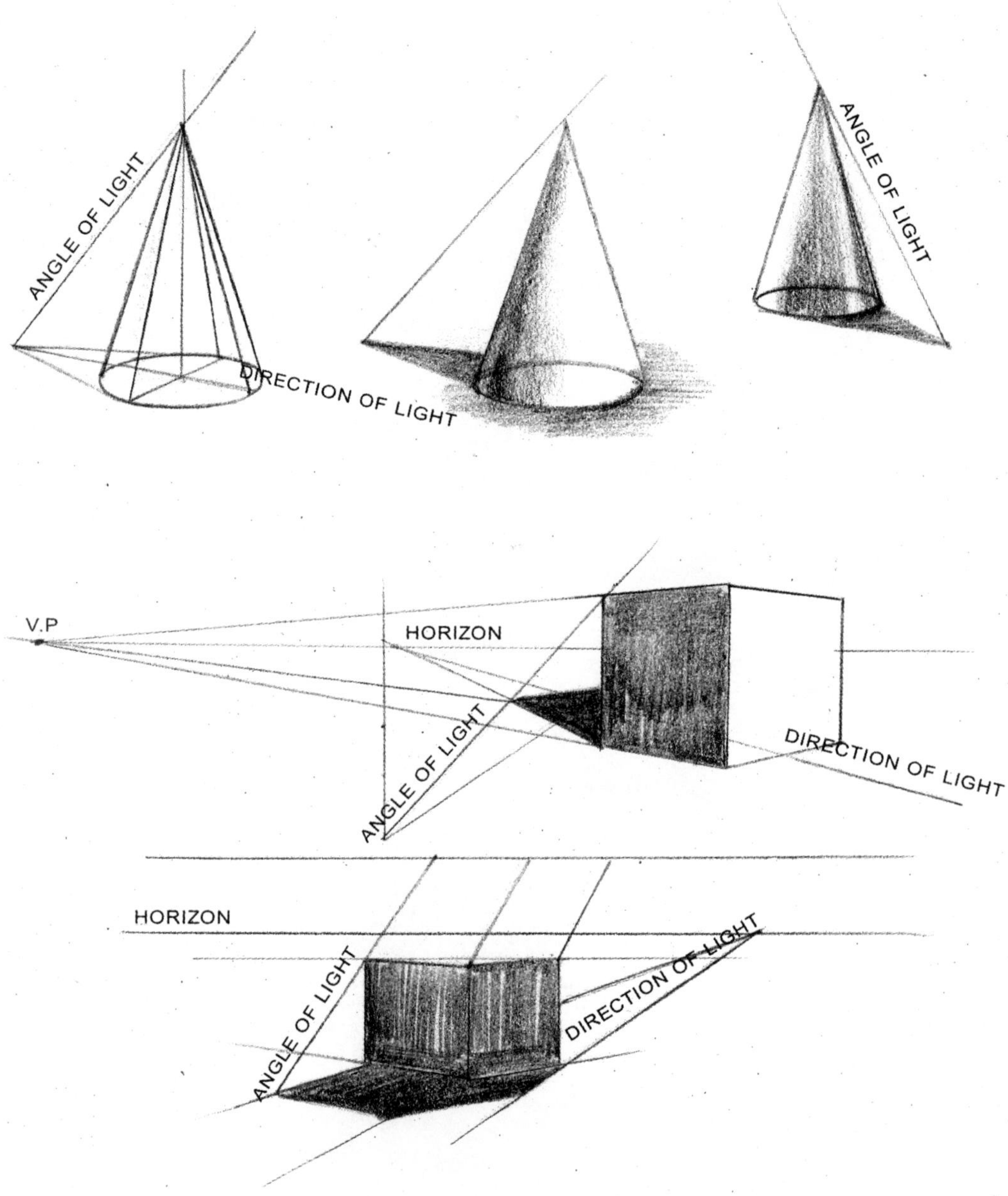

Light

It is the vital part of still life drawing. We should have a basic knowledge of the light reflection by different shapes of objects. It also involves the basic knowledge of the material and texture of the object.

Source of Light

Shadow falls directly opposite to the actual light source, this also includes the actual creation of light source as well as the characteristics of light and the volume of the subject.

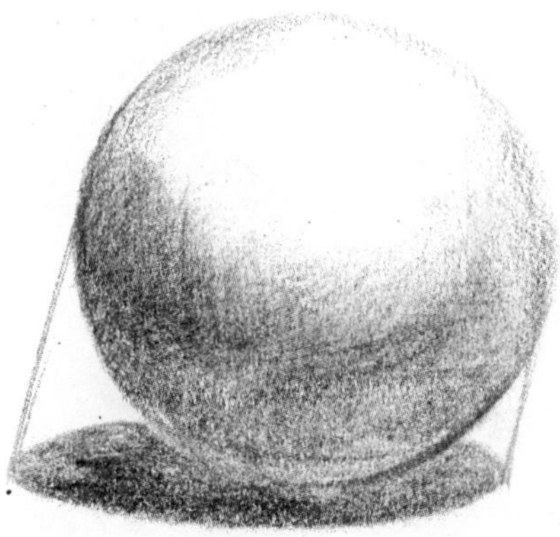

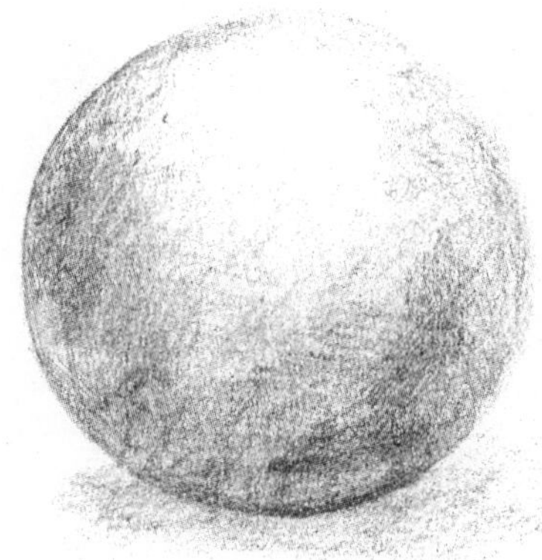

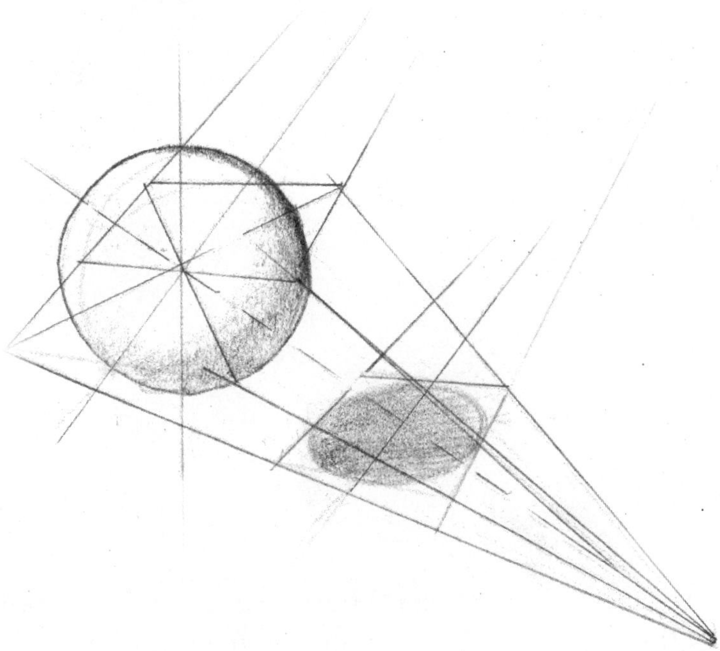

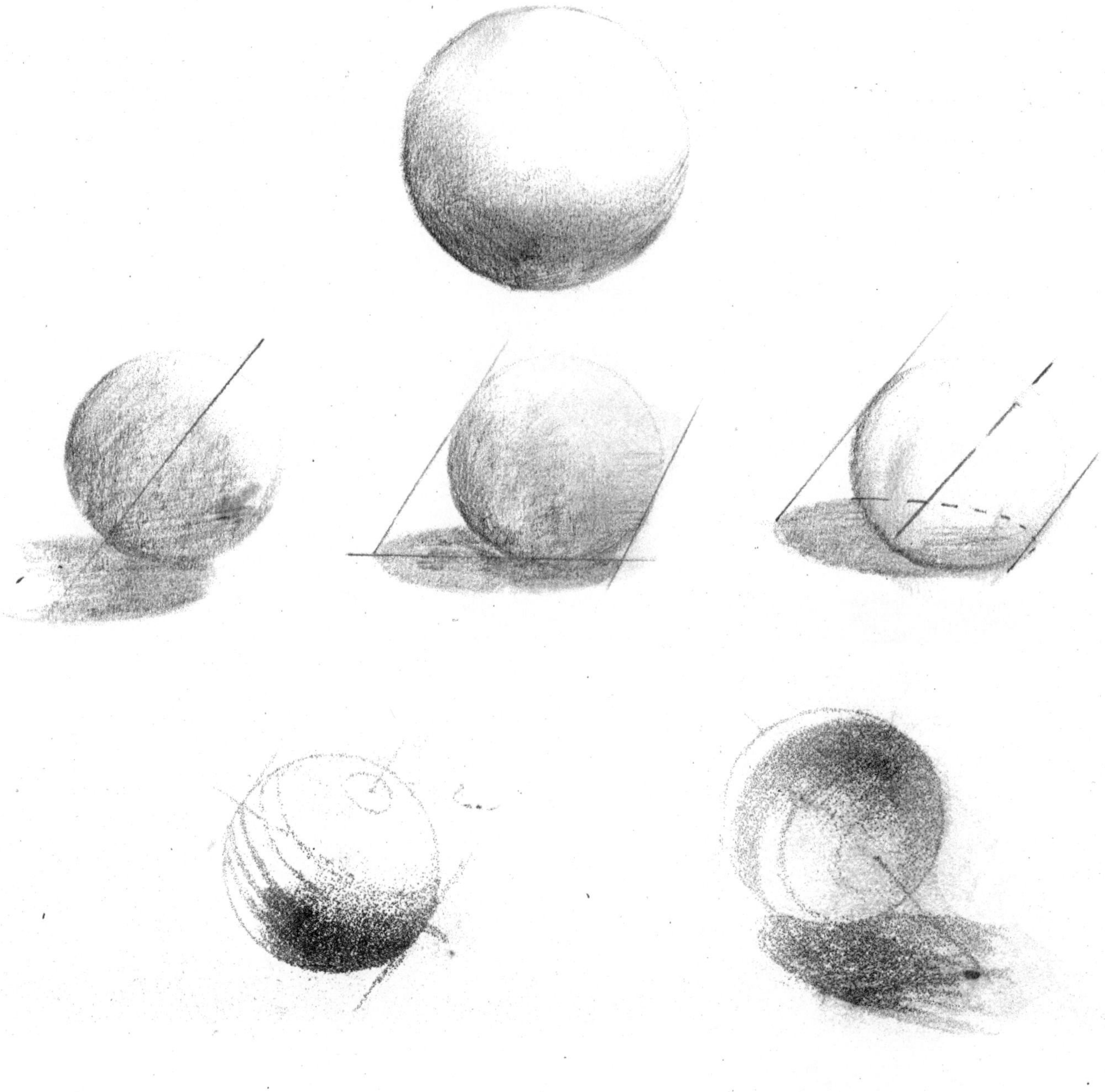

Light on the sphere

This is the bend of the darker shadow that appears between the half tone of the light and the reflected light within the shadow. The cast on the ground plane stretches from this bend.

Perspective of shadows

All shadows radiate from a point in the ground plane, directly beneath the light source. This is called the vanishing point of shadows, even though it is not on the horizon. Such shadows do not diminish as they recede towards the horizon.

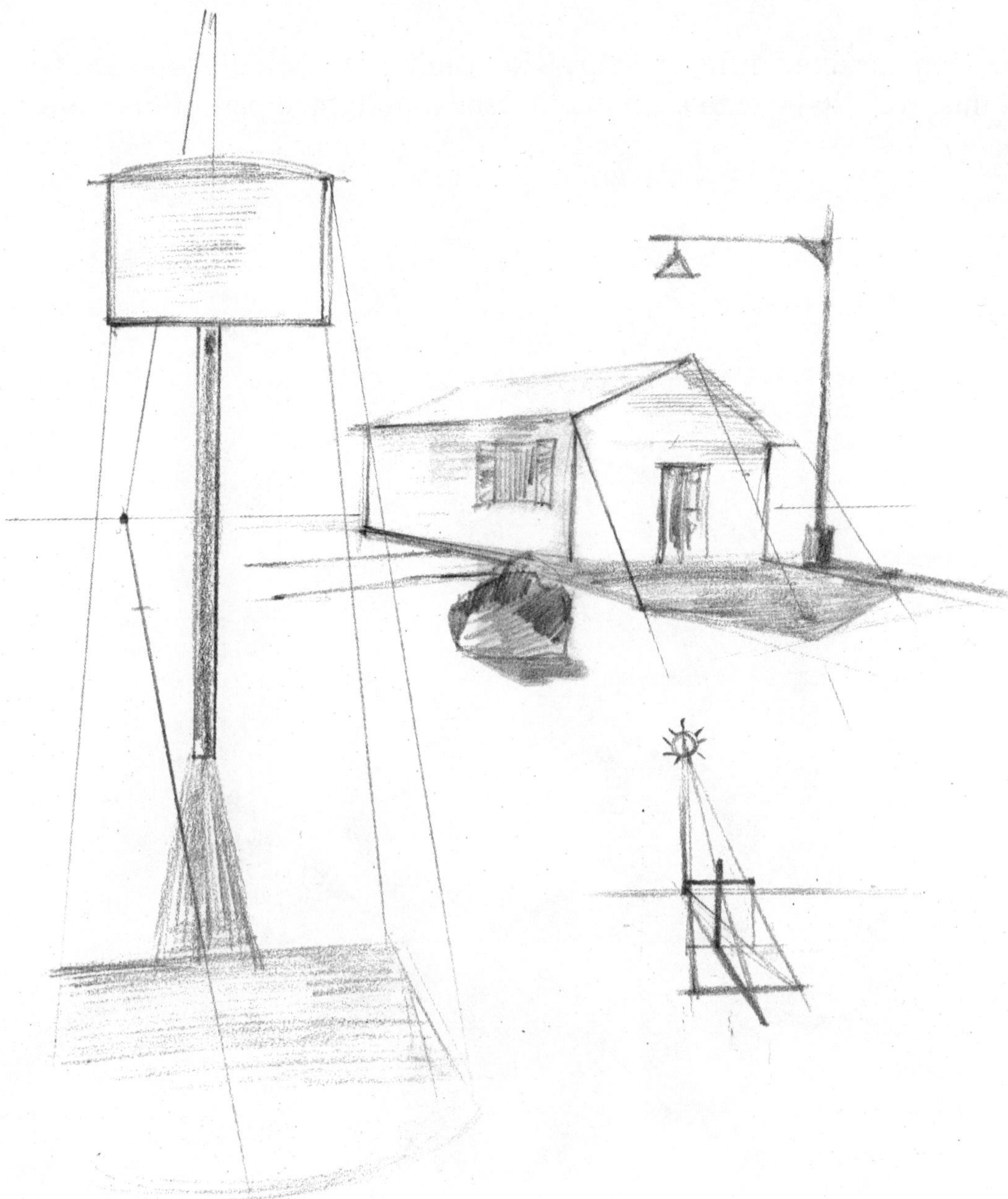

Tone Drawing

Tone Drawing involves the usage of light effect as well as the three dimensional aspects of still life drawing. It also brings out the photographic reality. This also helps you to gradually find out the colour of particular objects.

Tone drawing has three different stages, i.e. Light tone, Middle tone and Dark tone. Besides this, we also have to keep in mind the highlighted part of the subject.

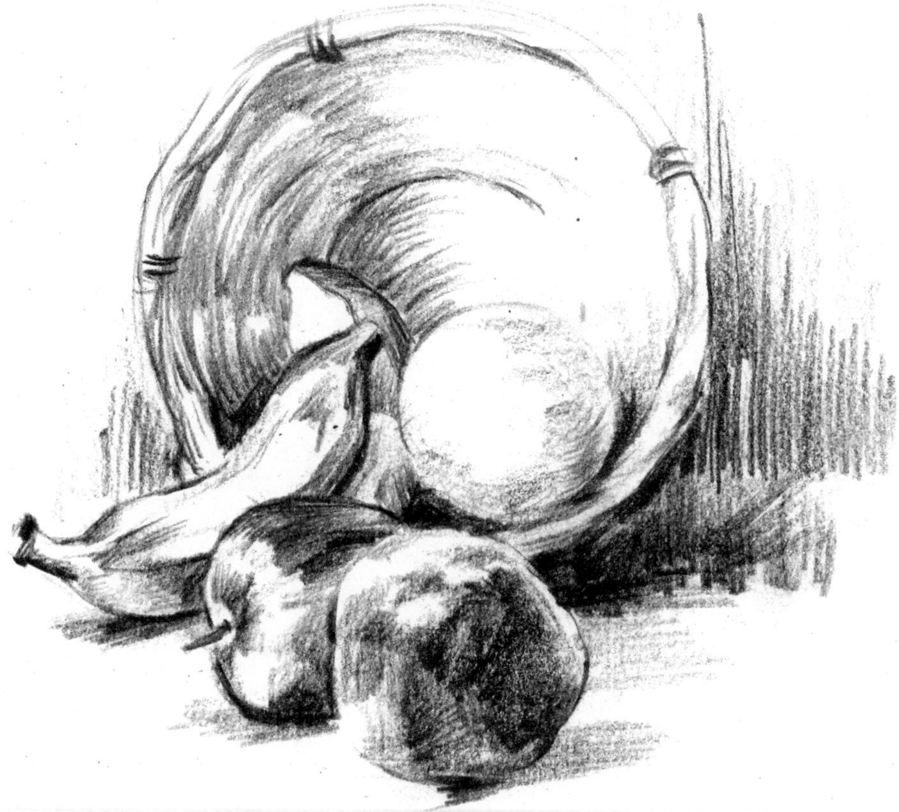

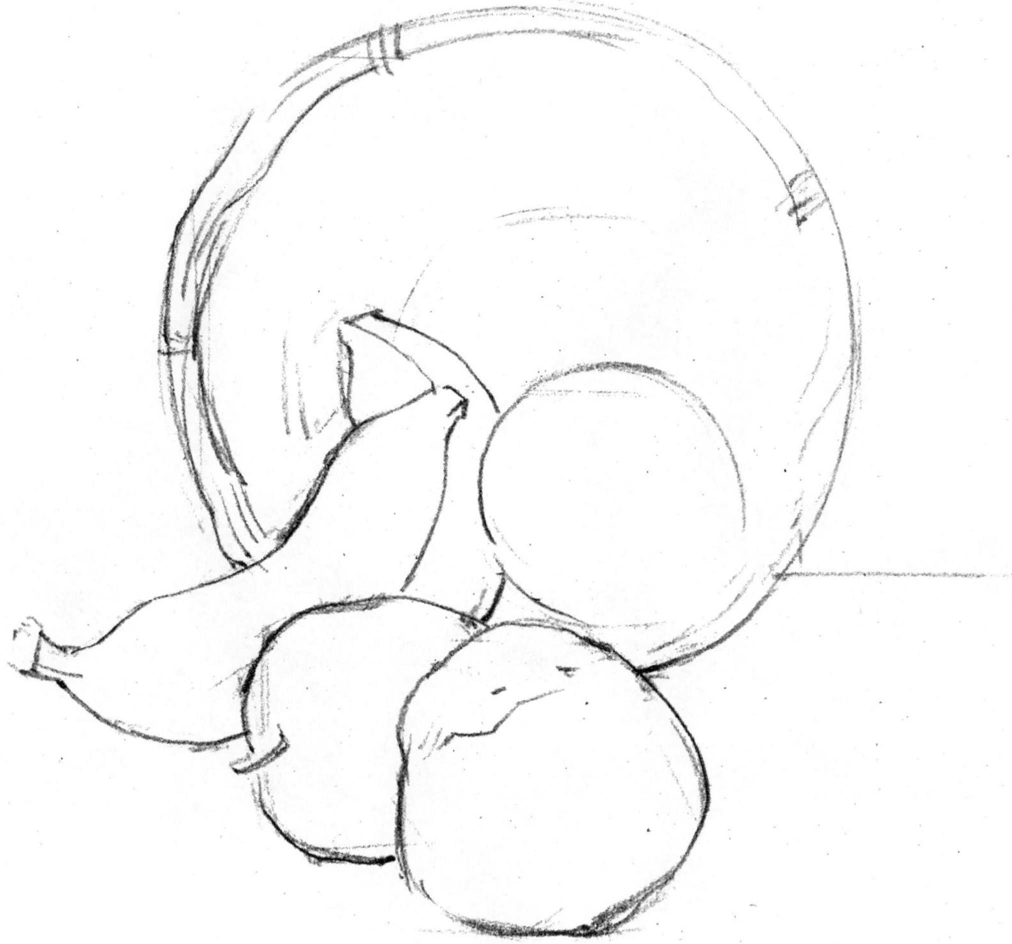

Line Drawing

To understand the basic elements of the subject we require line drawing. This makes us understand the elements of the subject and also its light and shade and volume properly. To search the basic aspects of drawing, line drawing plays a vital role.

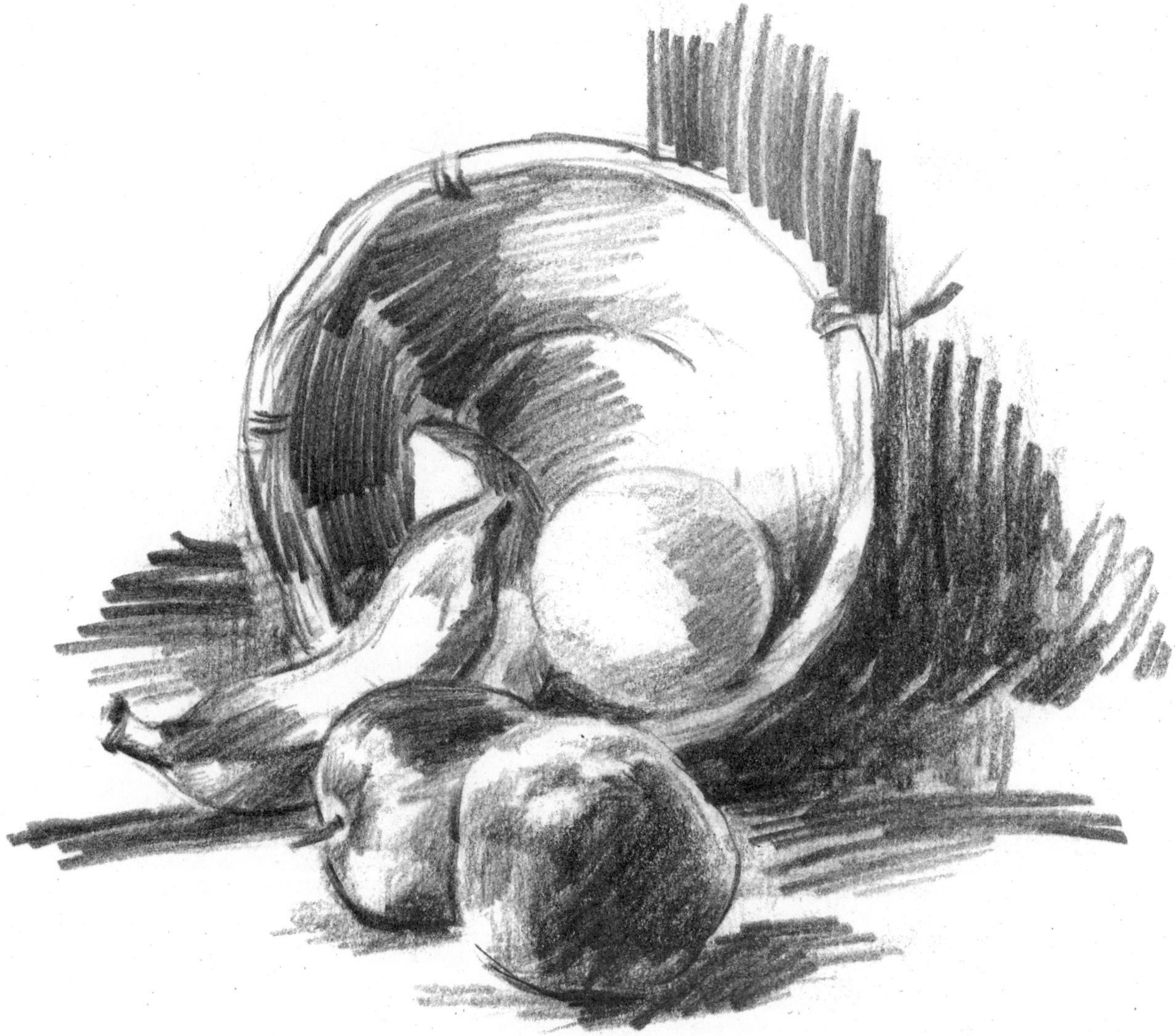

Constructive Drawing

It is the framework of still life drawing. While starting a still life drawing, constructive drawing makes us able to understand the actual geometrical shapes of the objects properly. It also helps in understanding the arrangement, subject placement, highlight and composition of the subject. These techniques are also used in the preparatory drawings for sculpture.

Structural Drawing

In part, this technique uses the same principles as used in constructive drawing, but in case of structural drawing, the expression of drawing is different. This involves the powerful effect of three dimensional aspects as well as it makes easy to understand the volume and light dimension.

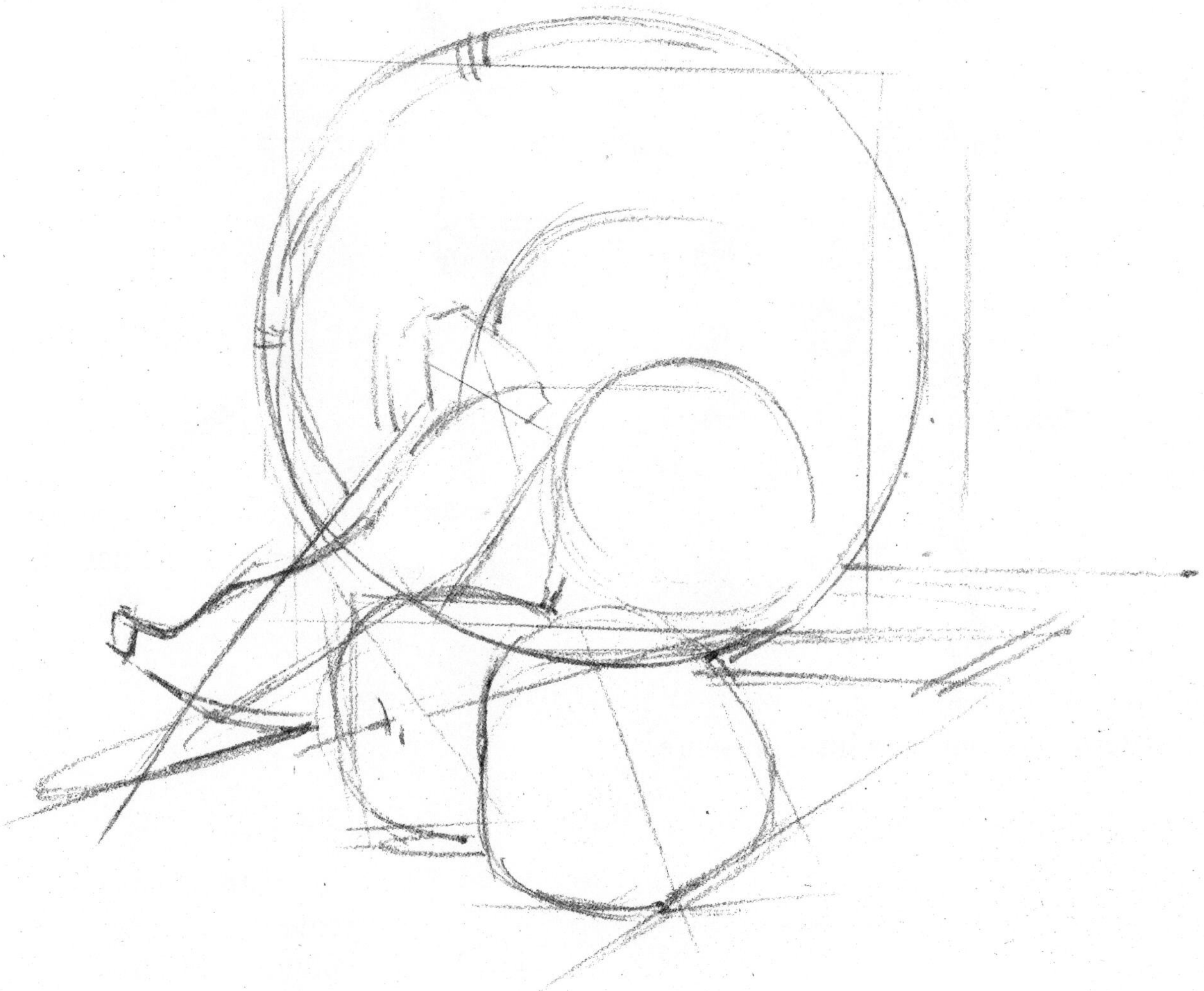

Lines & Strokes

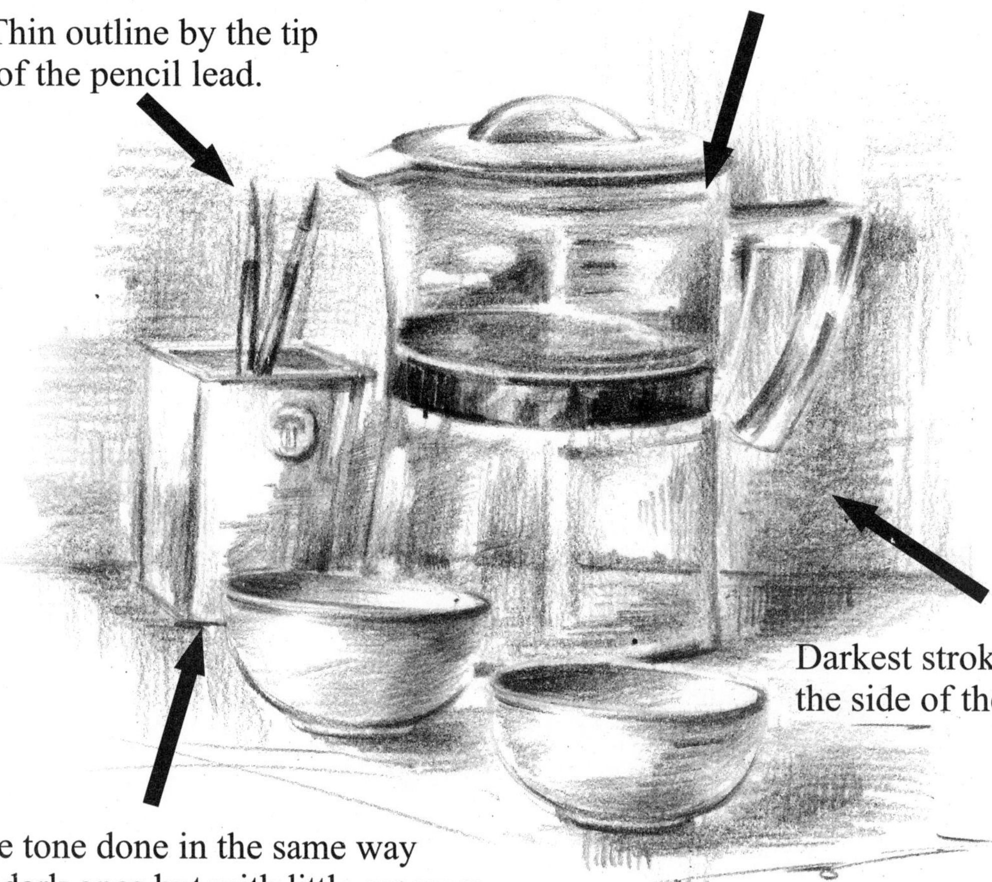

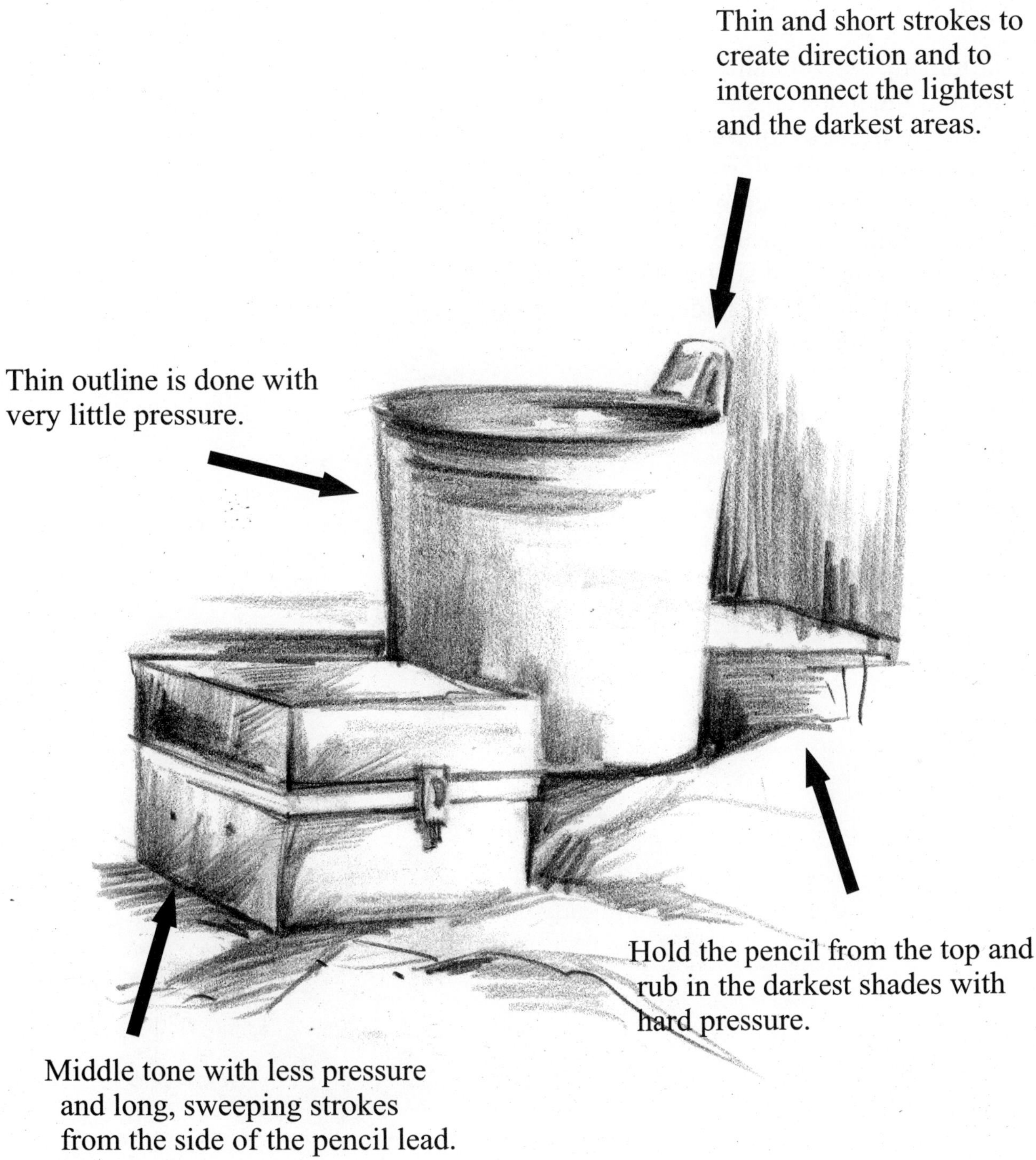
Thin and short strokes to create direction and to interconnect the lightest and the darkest areas.
Thin outline is done with very little pressure.
Hold the pencil from the top and rub in the darkest shades with hard pressure.
Middle tone with less pressure and long, sweeping strokes from the side of the pencil lead.

Stroke

The relationship between the variation of stroke and the material's texture is very important because the variation of stroke and its character brings out the subject properly. Here in case of the basket, the variation of stroke has been created using its light and shade. Also by using step-by-step dark shade, the curvature of the subject has been brought out. Here the direction of the stroke is moved horizontally and vertically.

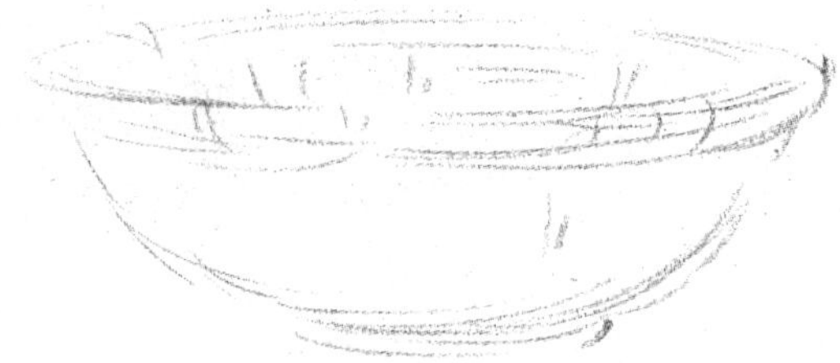

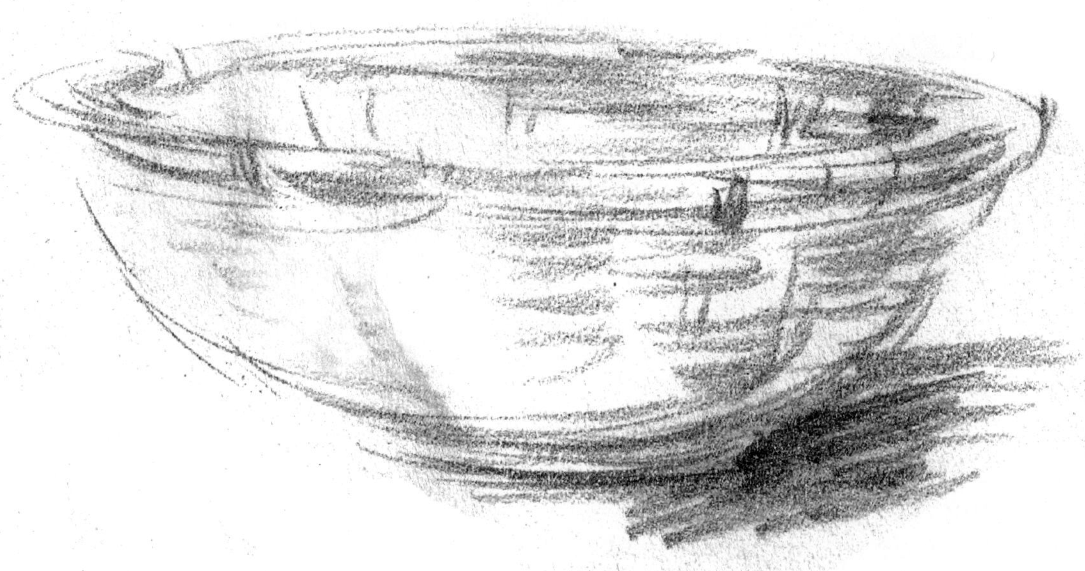

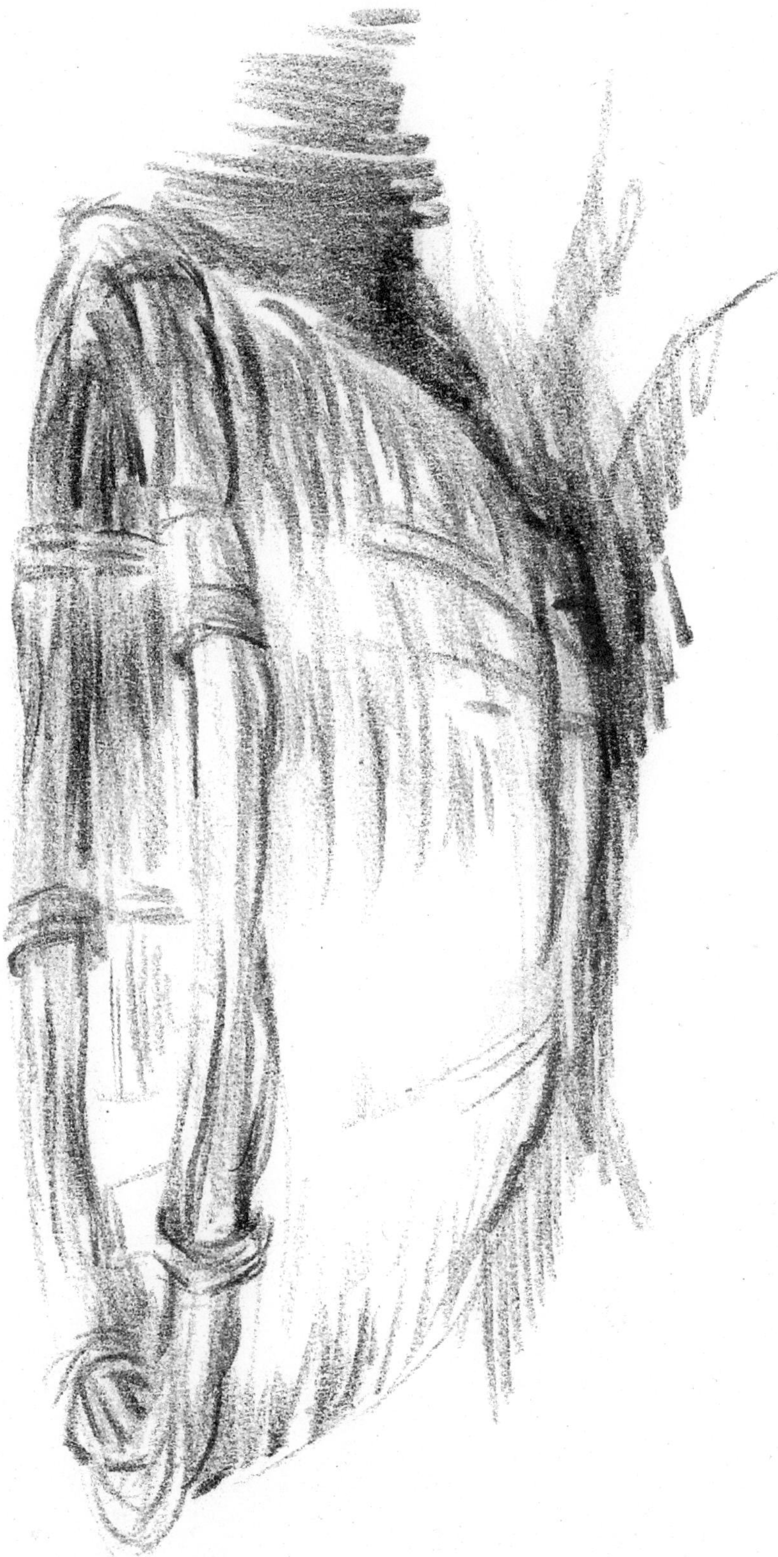

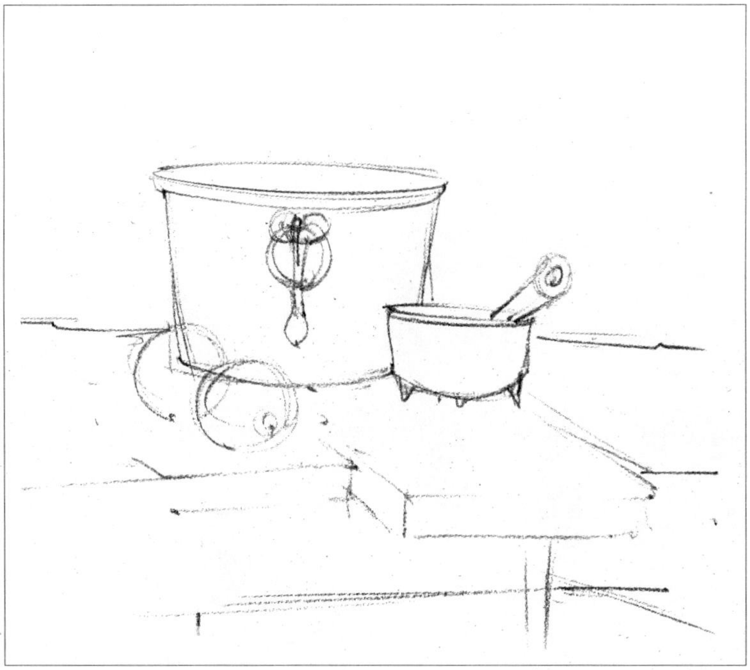

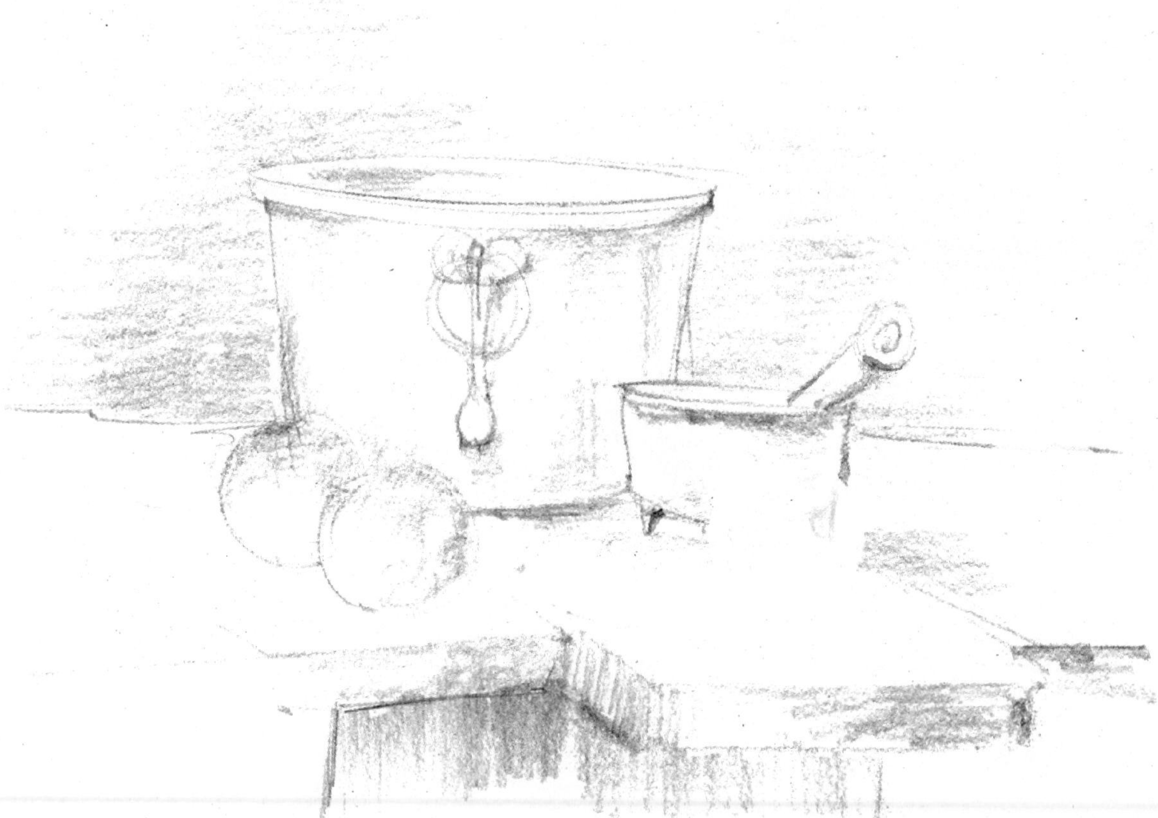

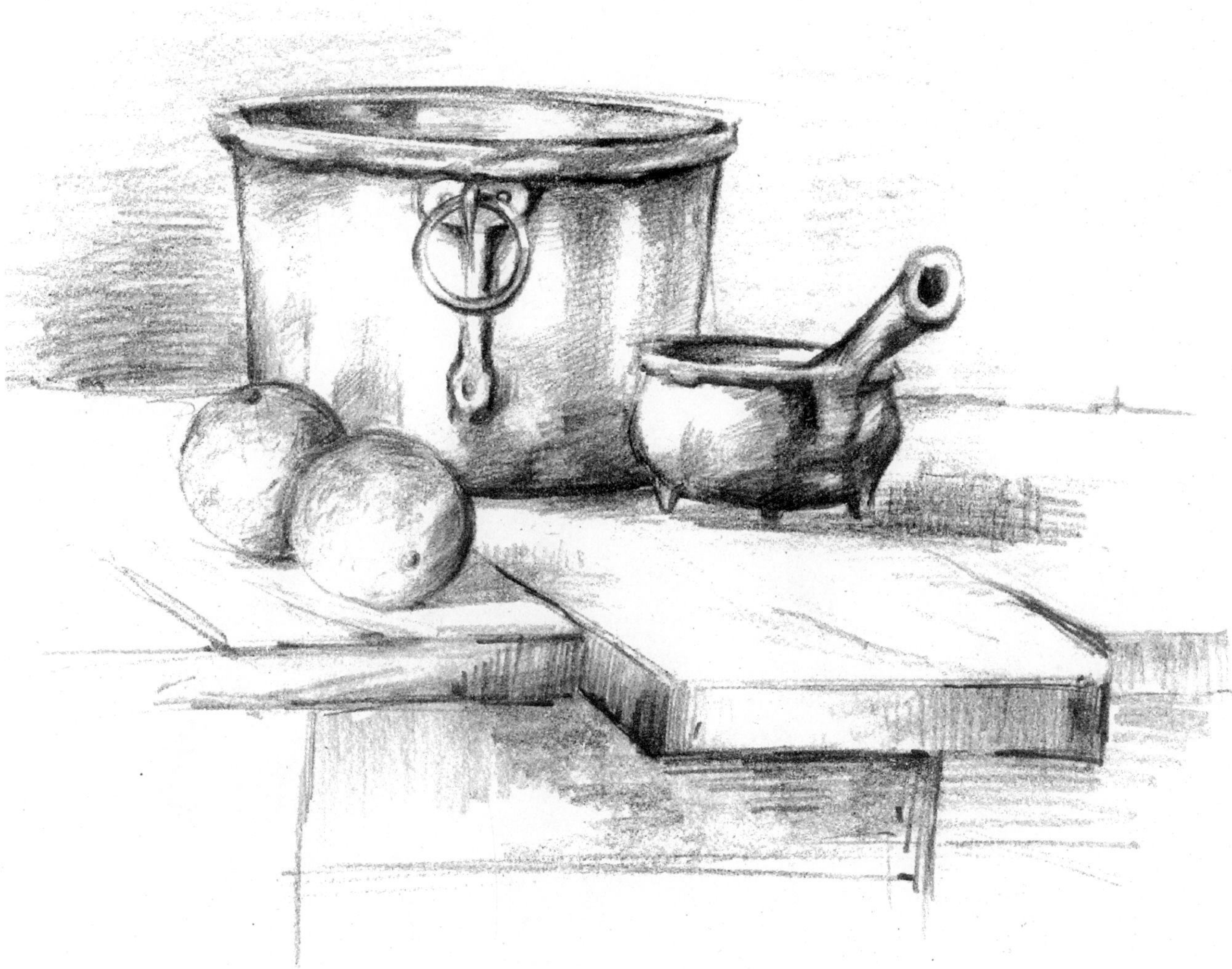

Texture and the curvatures of a certain part change with the view and you should be able to capture that difference.

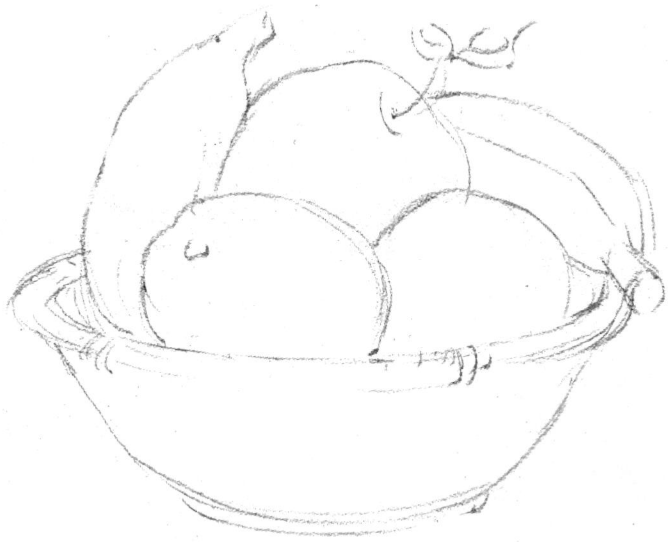

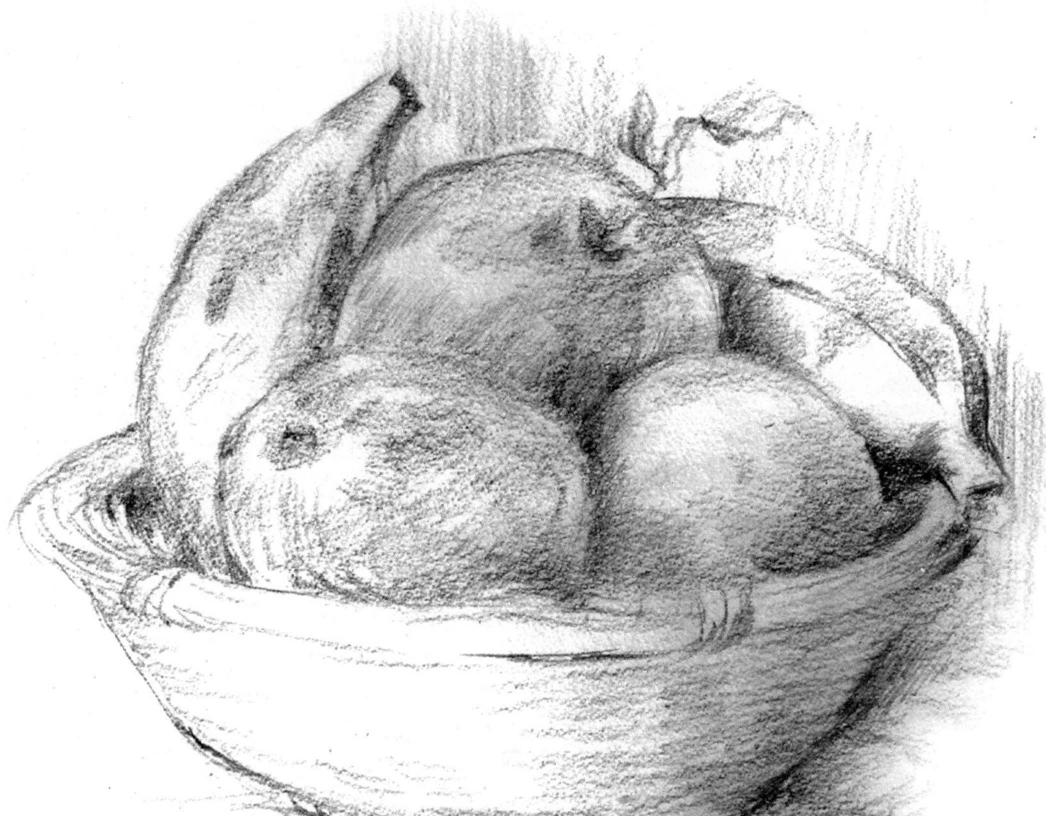

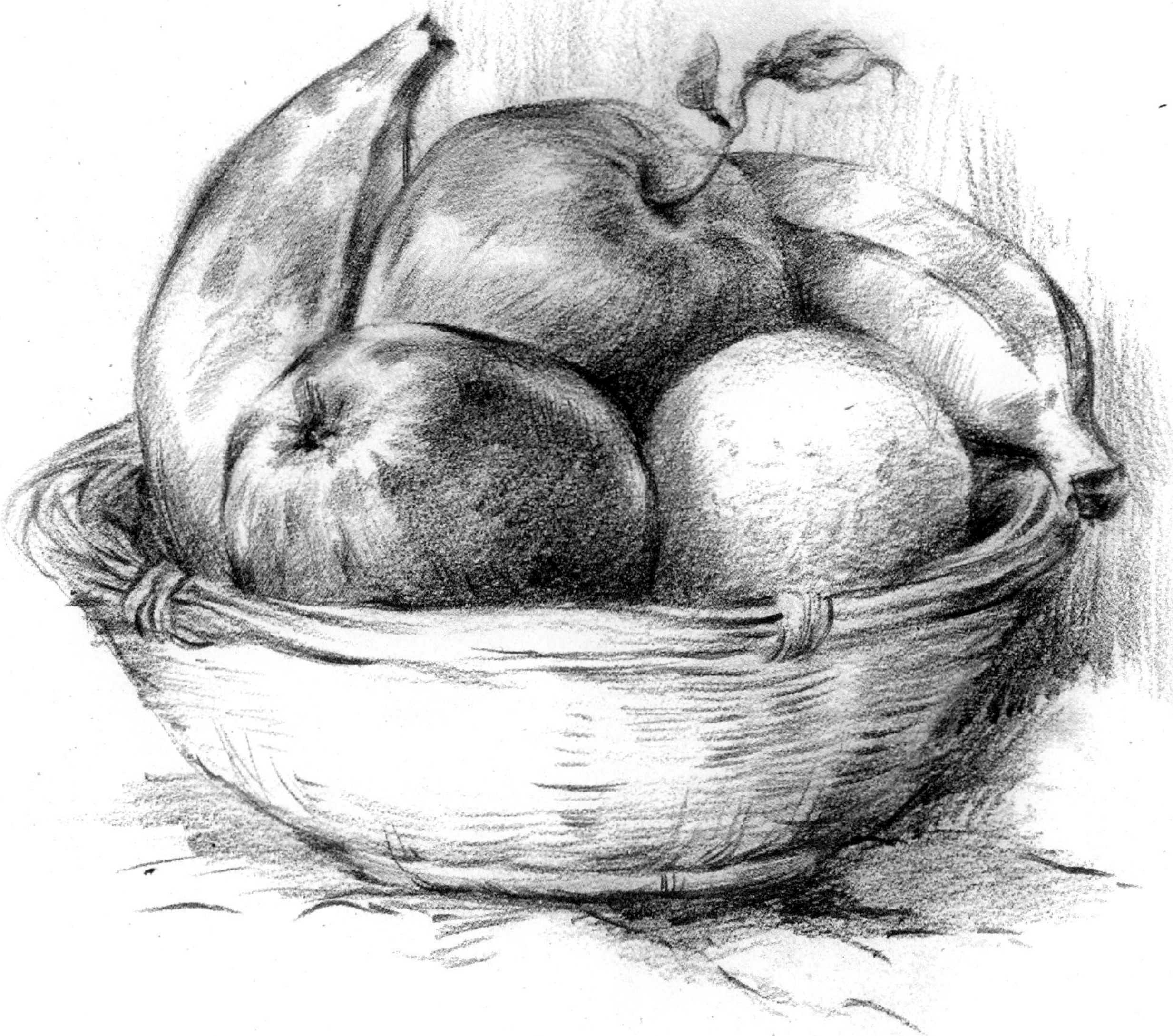

In the plastic jar above, we have used pencil's pressure softly to give volume to it. After this, the highlighted part has been shown using the paper white, the material dark tone has been used to make it clearer.

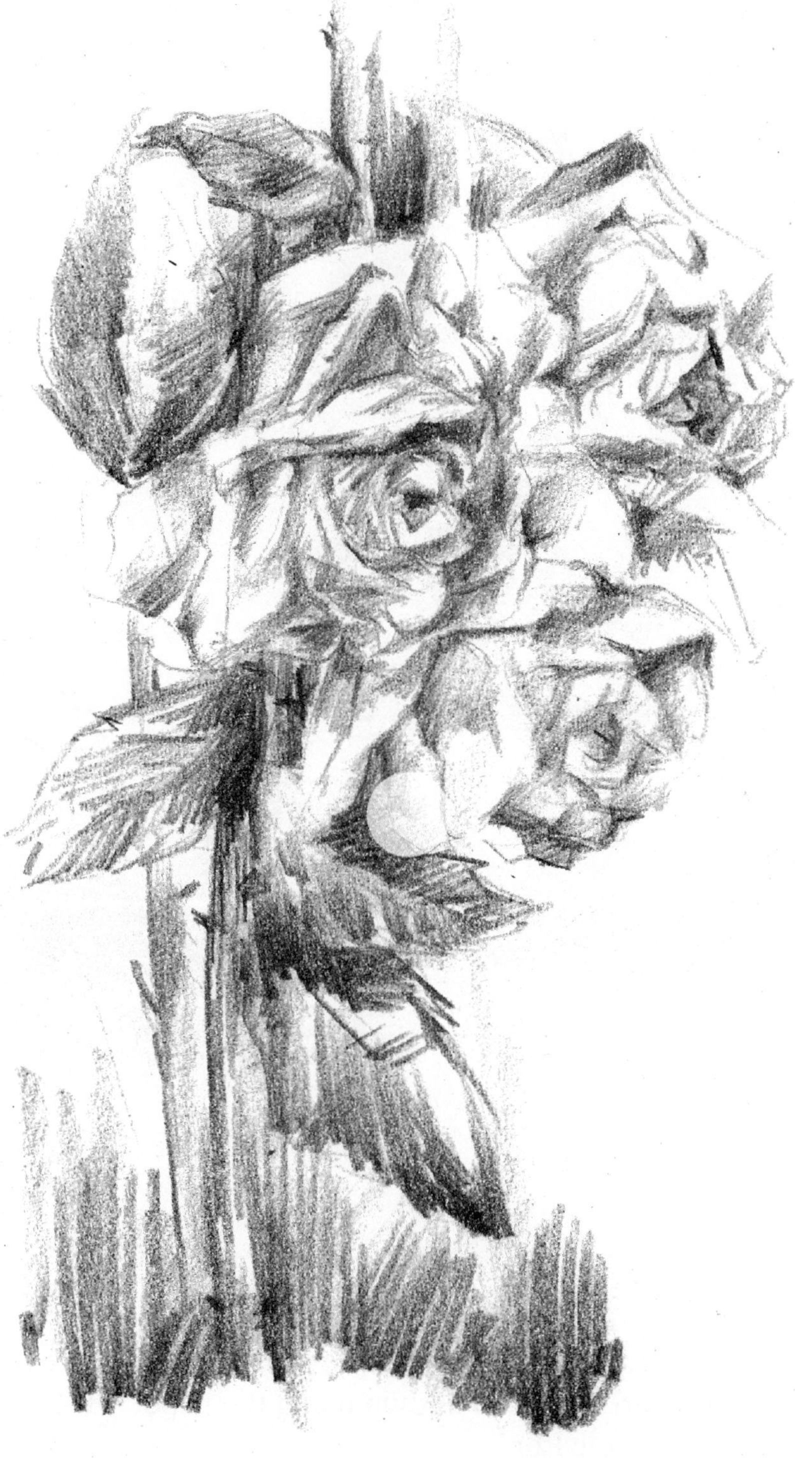

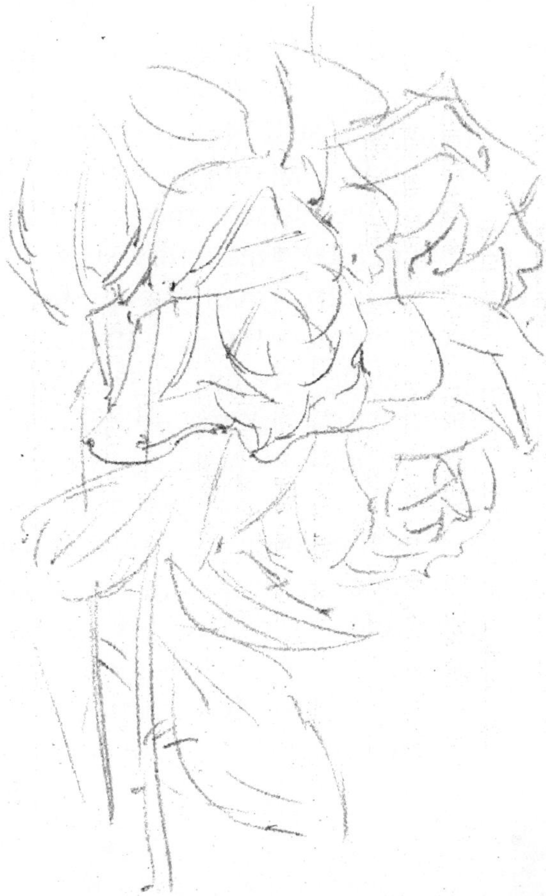

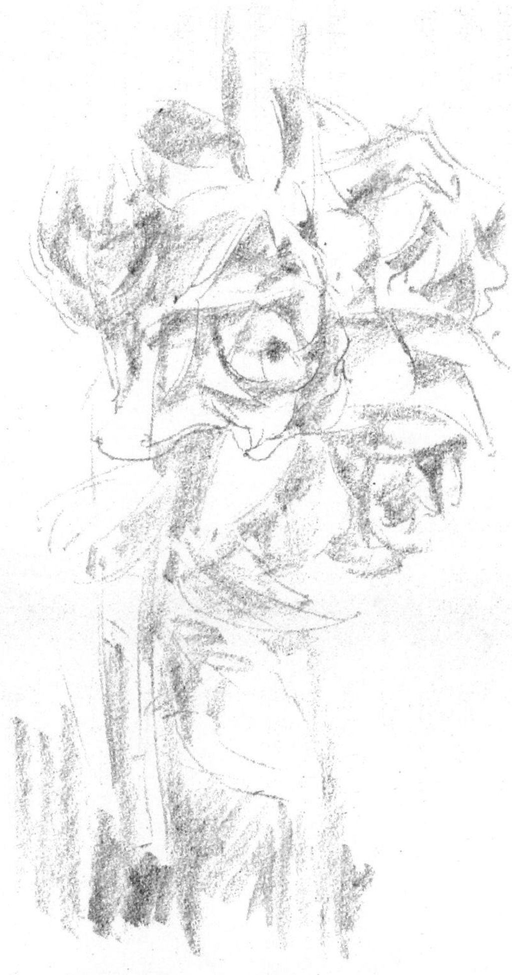

Flower

In this picture we will study how to give stroke to a rose flower. In the first step the thin line should be drawn properly. According to the direction of the light we will increase the pencil pressure. Here you can also use a small technique. The highlighted part can be erased neatly which will bring out the perfect character of the rose.

Egg

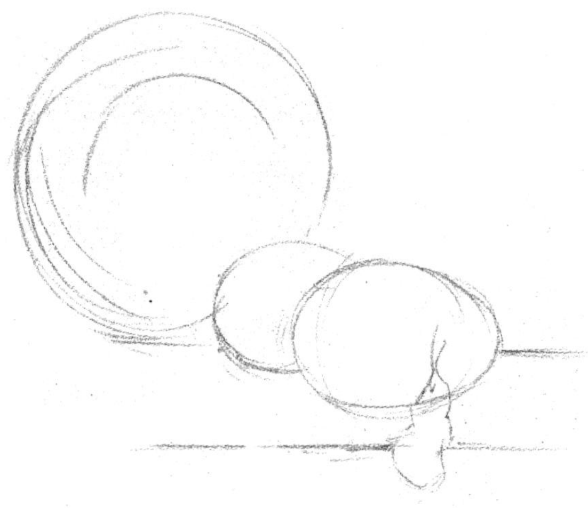

In case of still life study, the subject of egg is very much challenging. In the picture shown above, we need to understand a step-by-step drawing process. By using thin line we can create the egg. In the second step we have used dark tone to give the background, which brings out the character of the egg. After this by using pencil pressure softly, the volume of the egg has been shown. In the case of broken eggs and egg whites, giving pencil strokes is very challenging. By using proper light direction and pencil stroke movement we can bring out the egg white's shape.

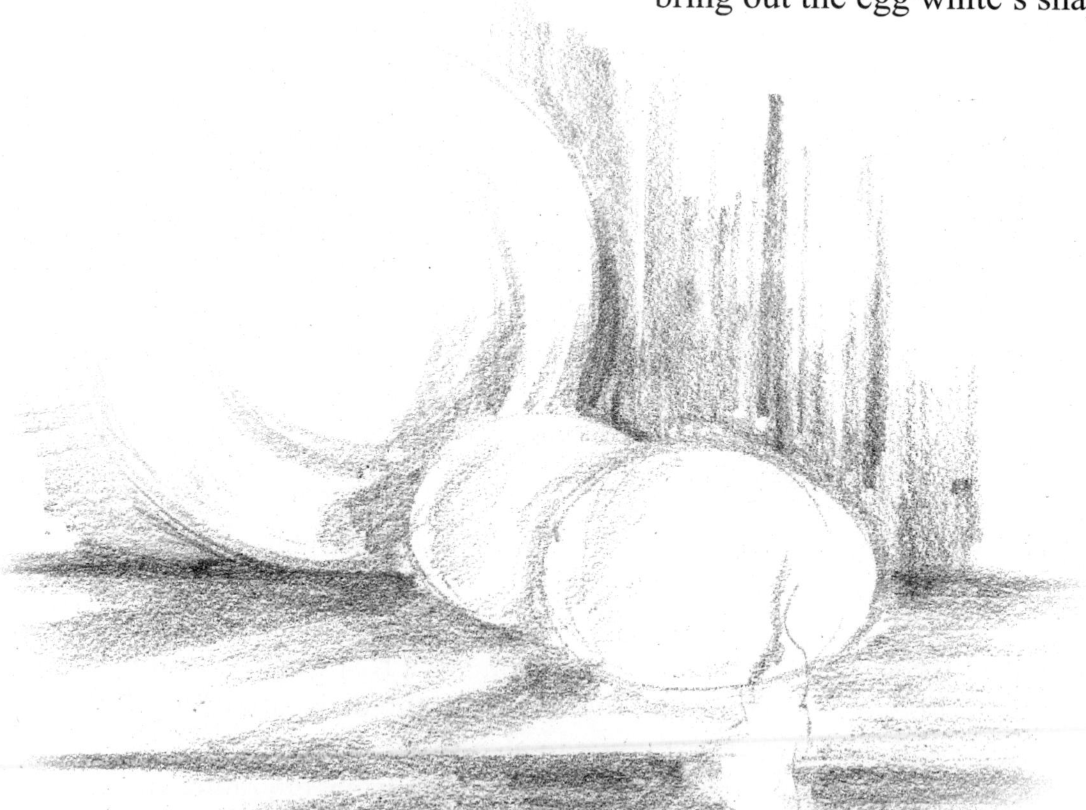

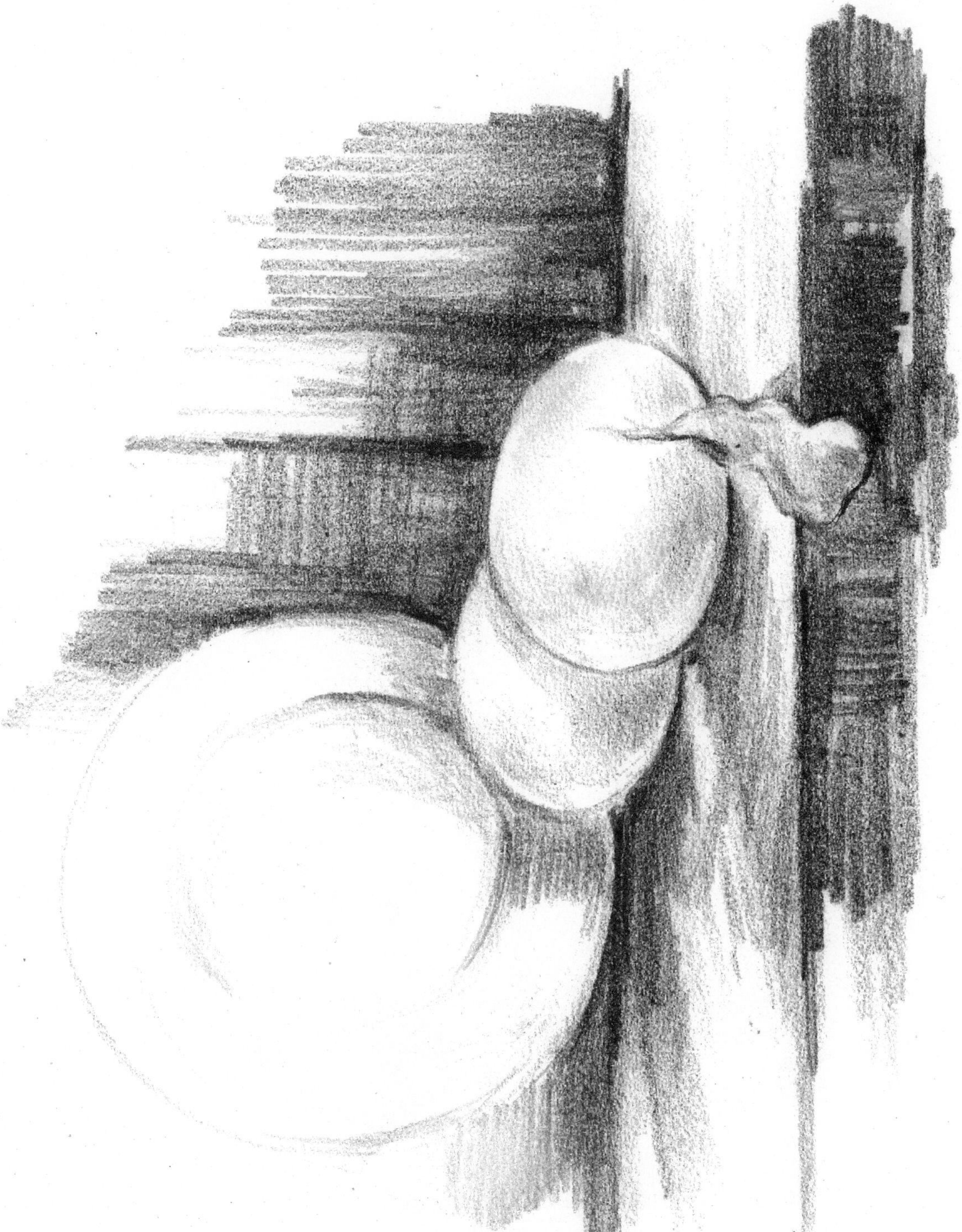

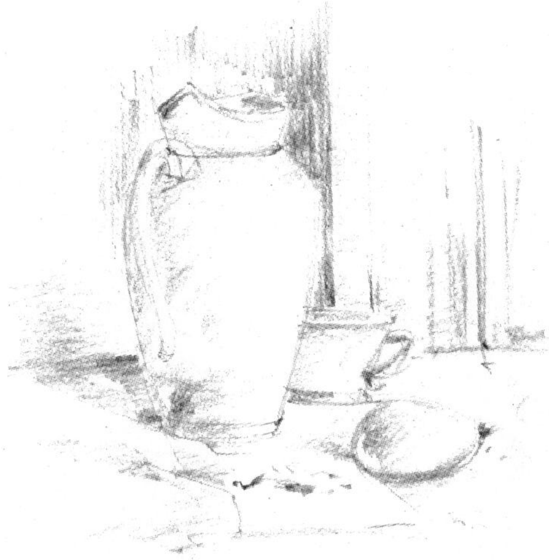

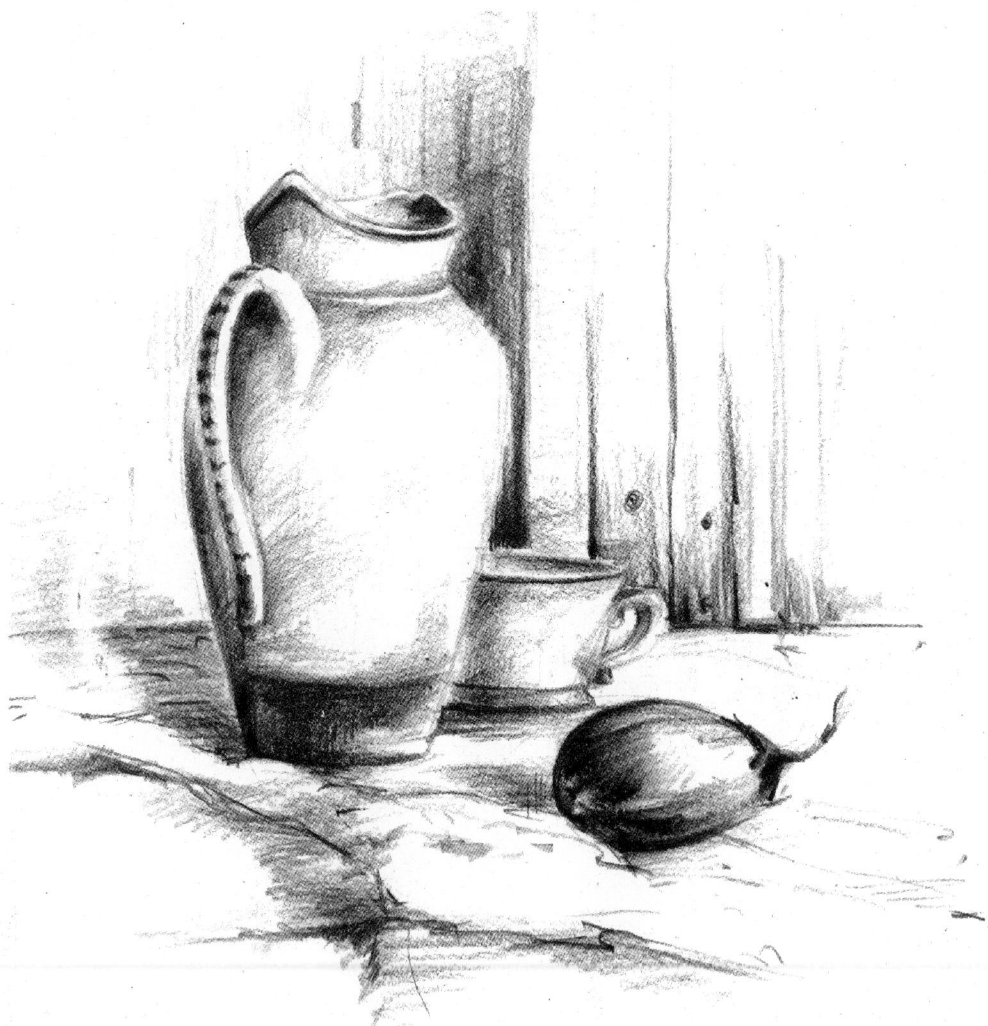

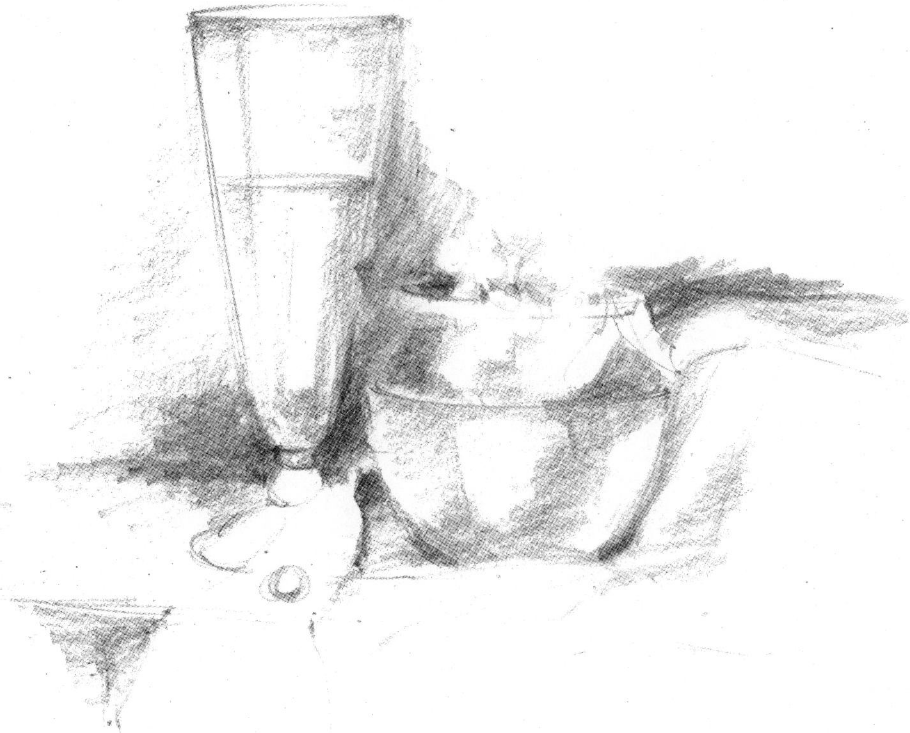

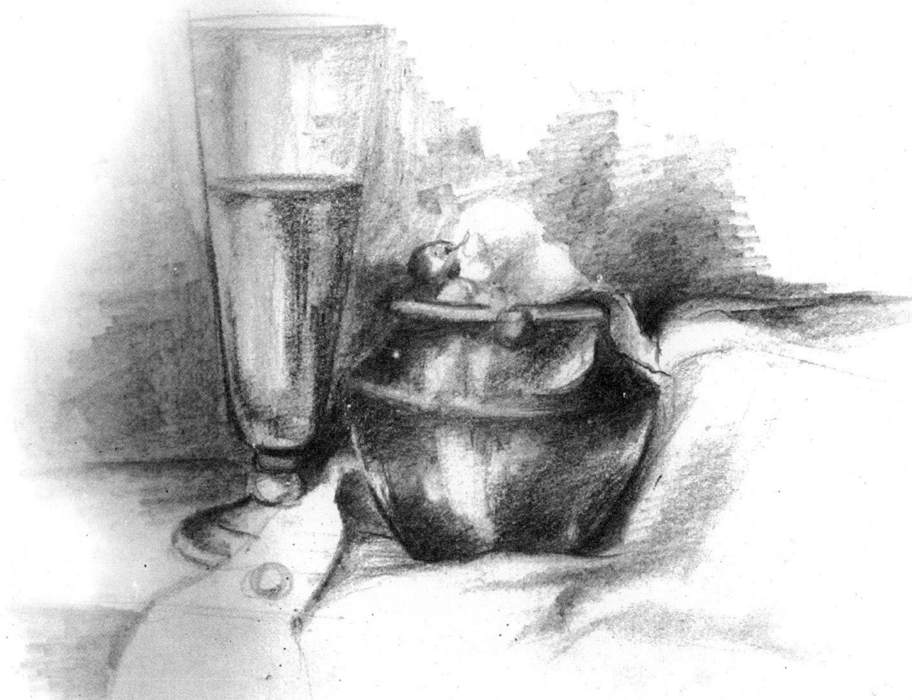

Once you get control on your pencil then the lines will be like melody. You can play and enjoy it as and when you wish.

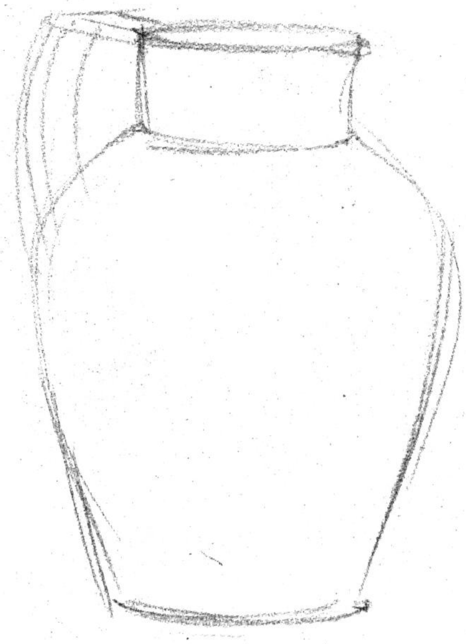

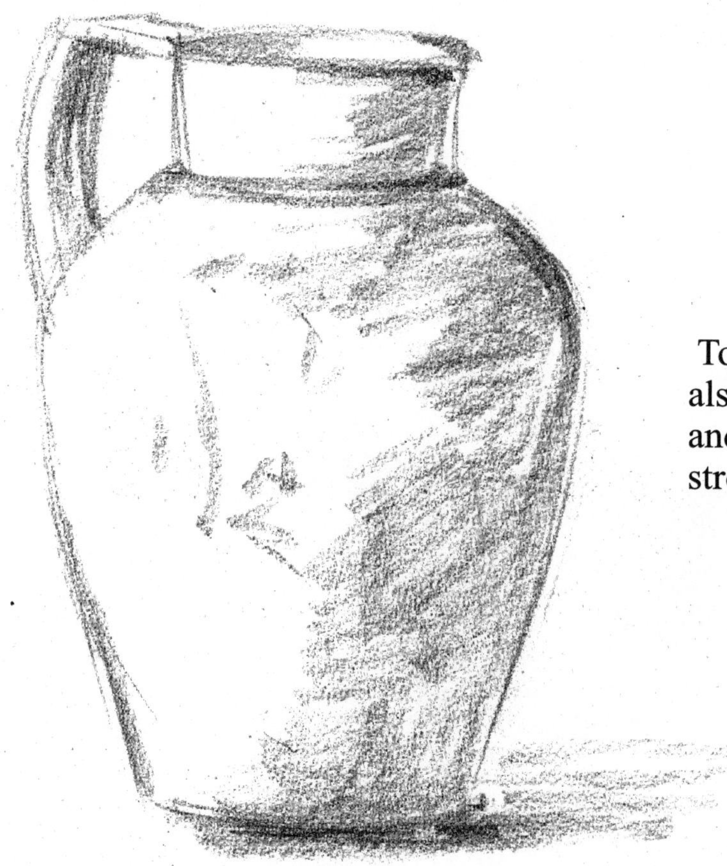

To understand the reflection we should also observe the subject's reflection and character. In case of reflection the strokes are used vertically.

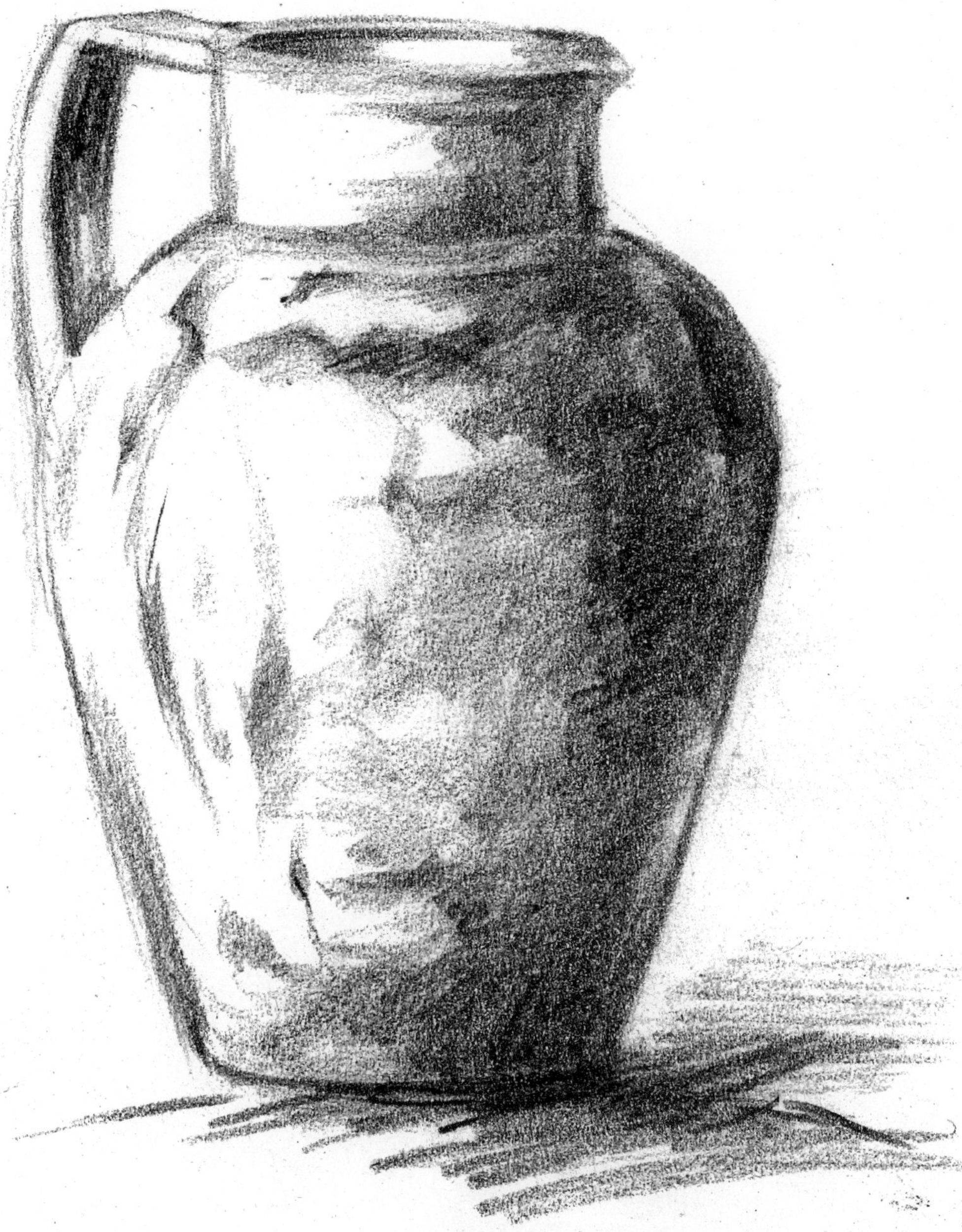

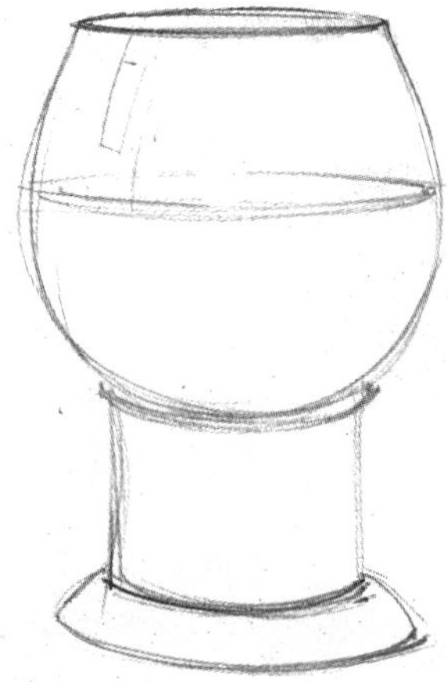

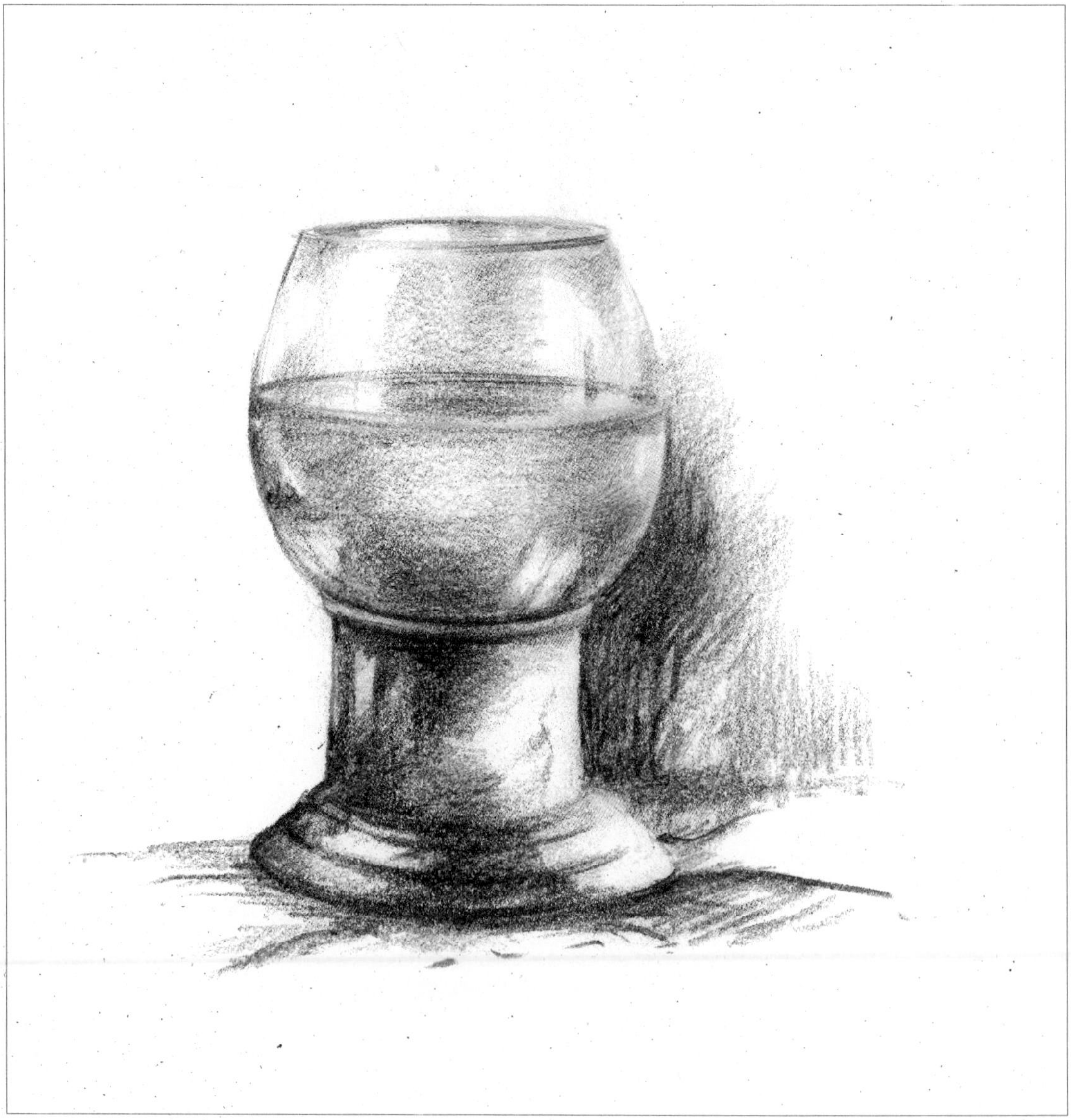

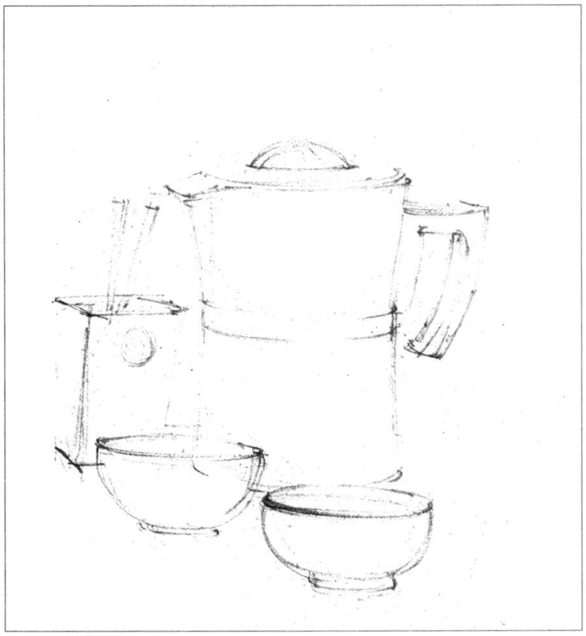

In this subject we can see three different individual elements. In the water jar to show its transparency, we have used light strokes in the first step, then in the second step, dark stroke and strokes dimension has been used to bring out the character of the subject. Here in the two bowls we have used round strokes equally.

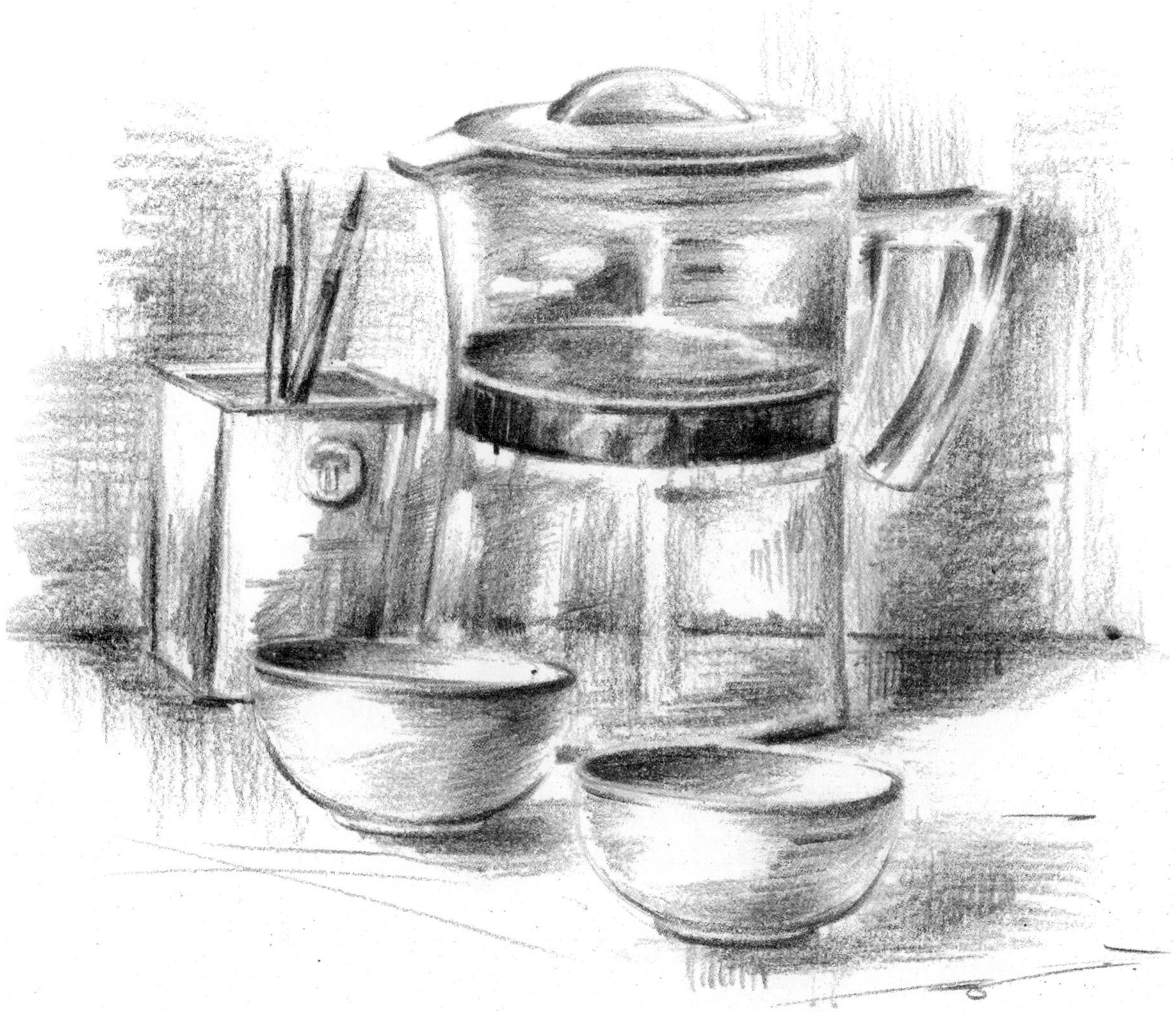

Apple

A proper view of this picture can show the difference in the pencil strokes that have been used. Firstly, the apple was drawn, then according to the source of light the basic pencil stroke is being given. After this, in case of direction of the apple, the stroke's dimension and by using thick line we created the volume of the apple. In case of drawing the banana the same procedure has been used. As both their shapes are different, so is their direction.

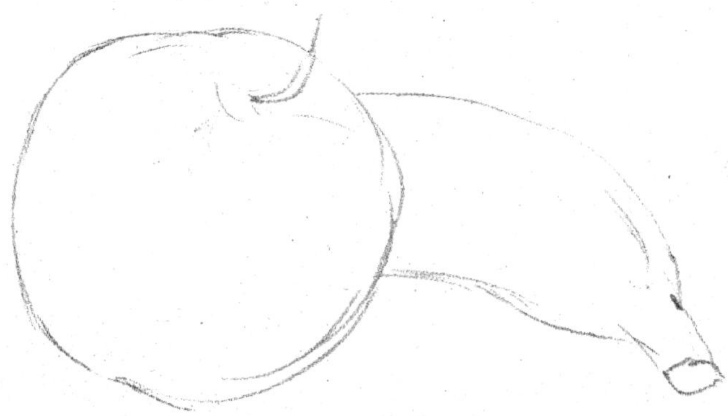

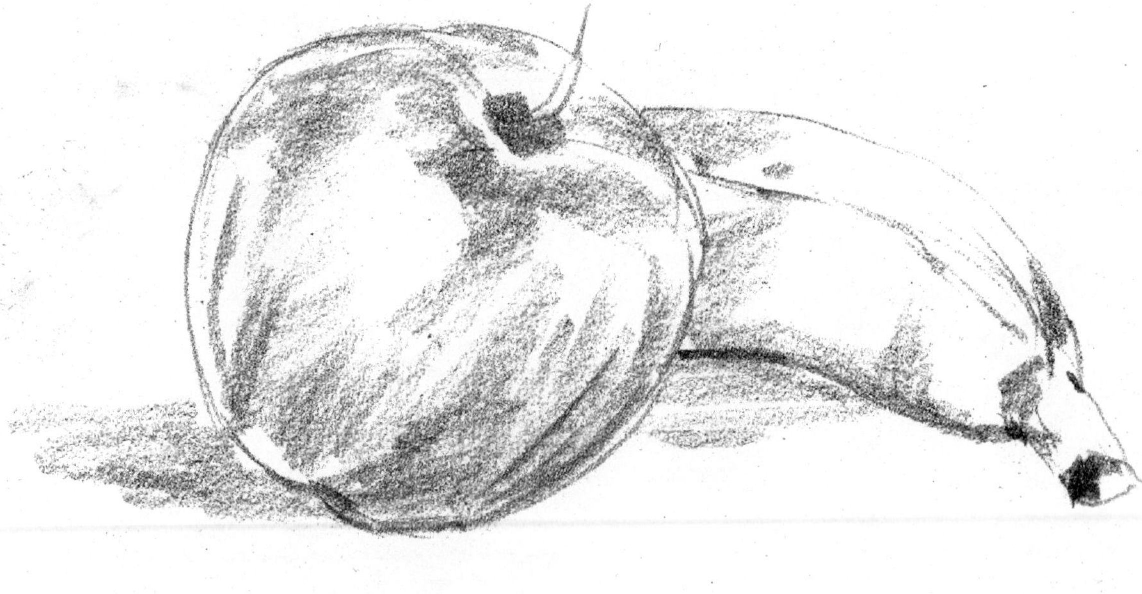

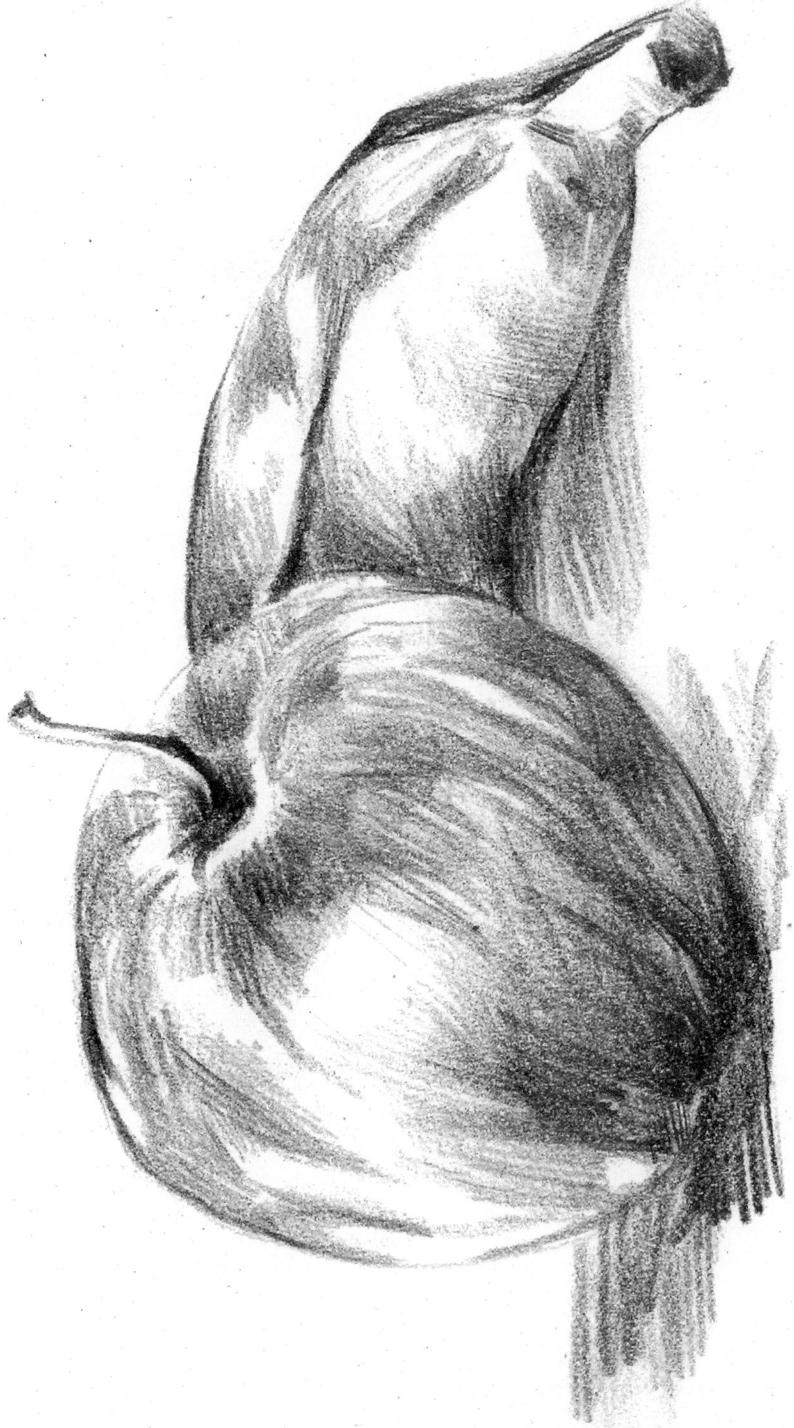

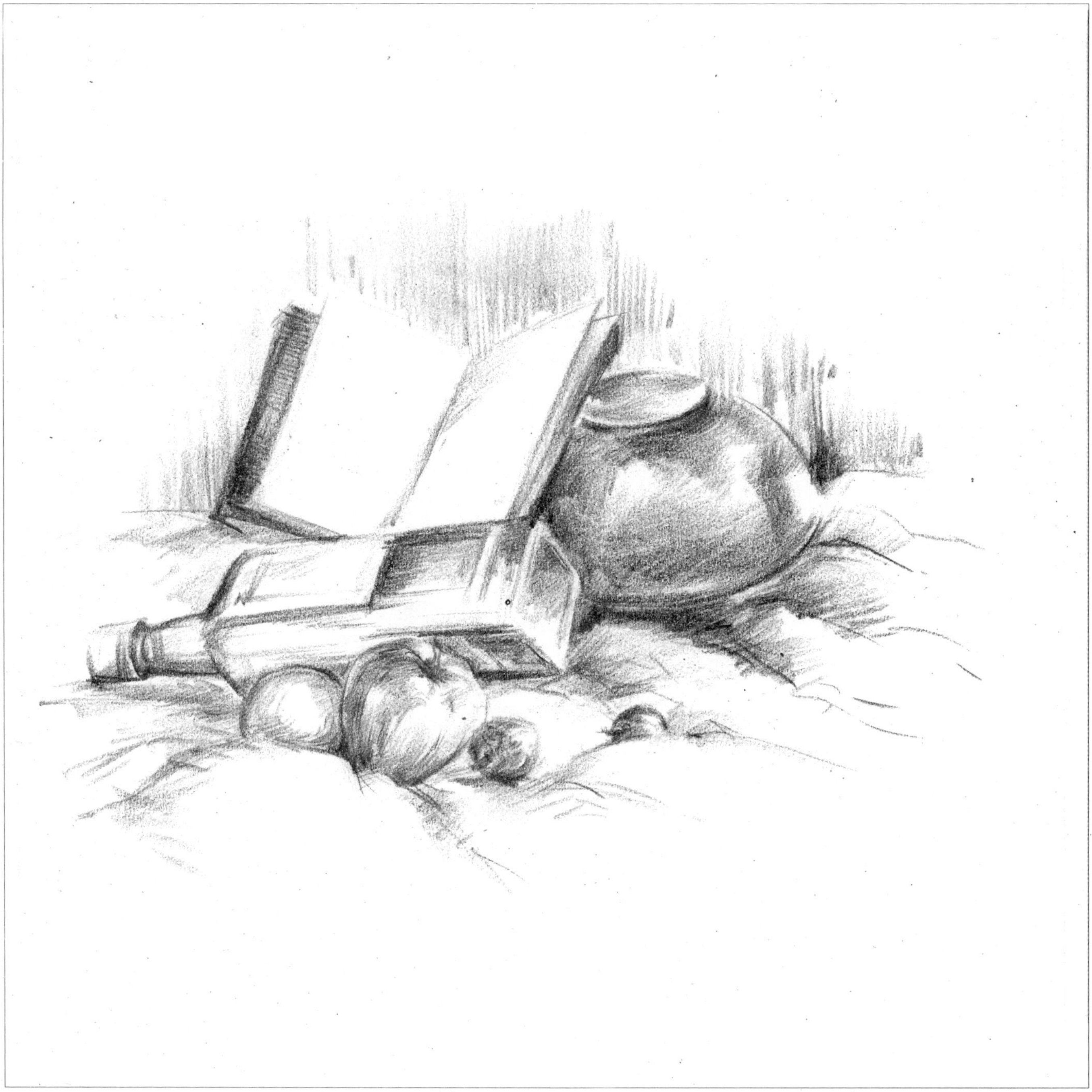

In many cases, still life brings us near to many new challenges. In this drawing, we will learn how to give strokes to different subject material, as every material's character is not always same. That's why the stroke pressure and direction depends on the material of the subject. Normally, according to the subject's volume, the stroke direction changes.

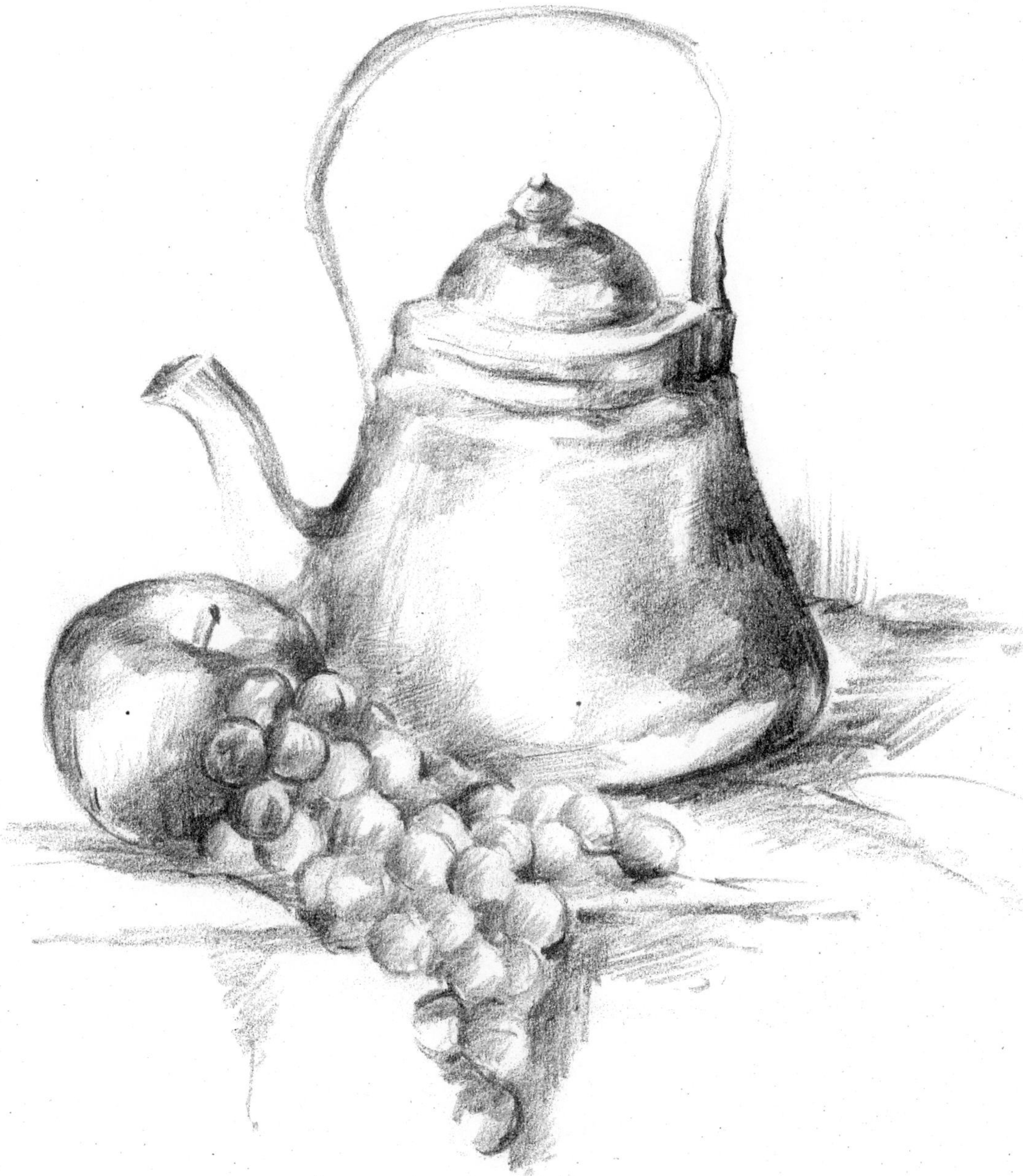

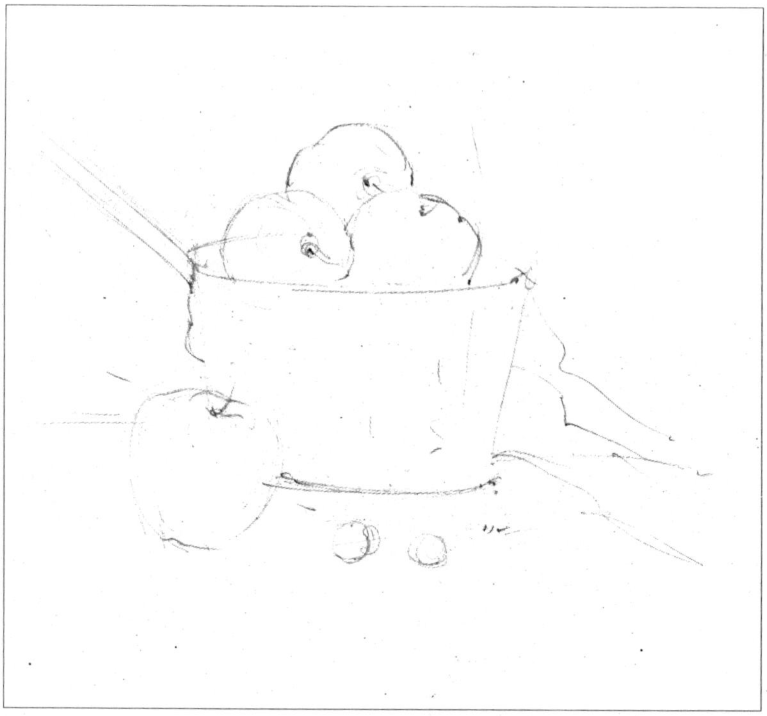

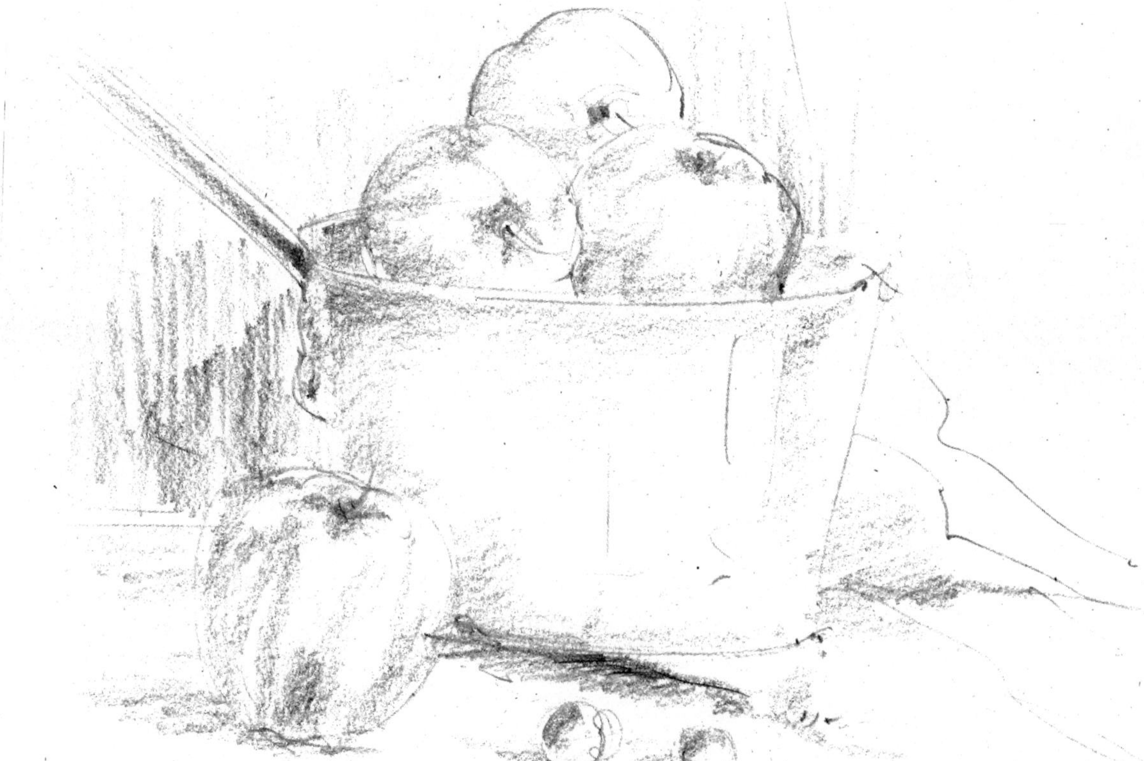

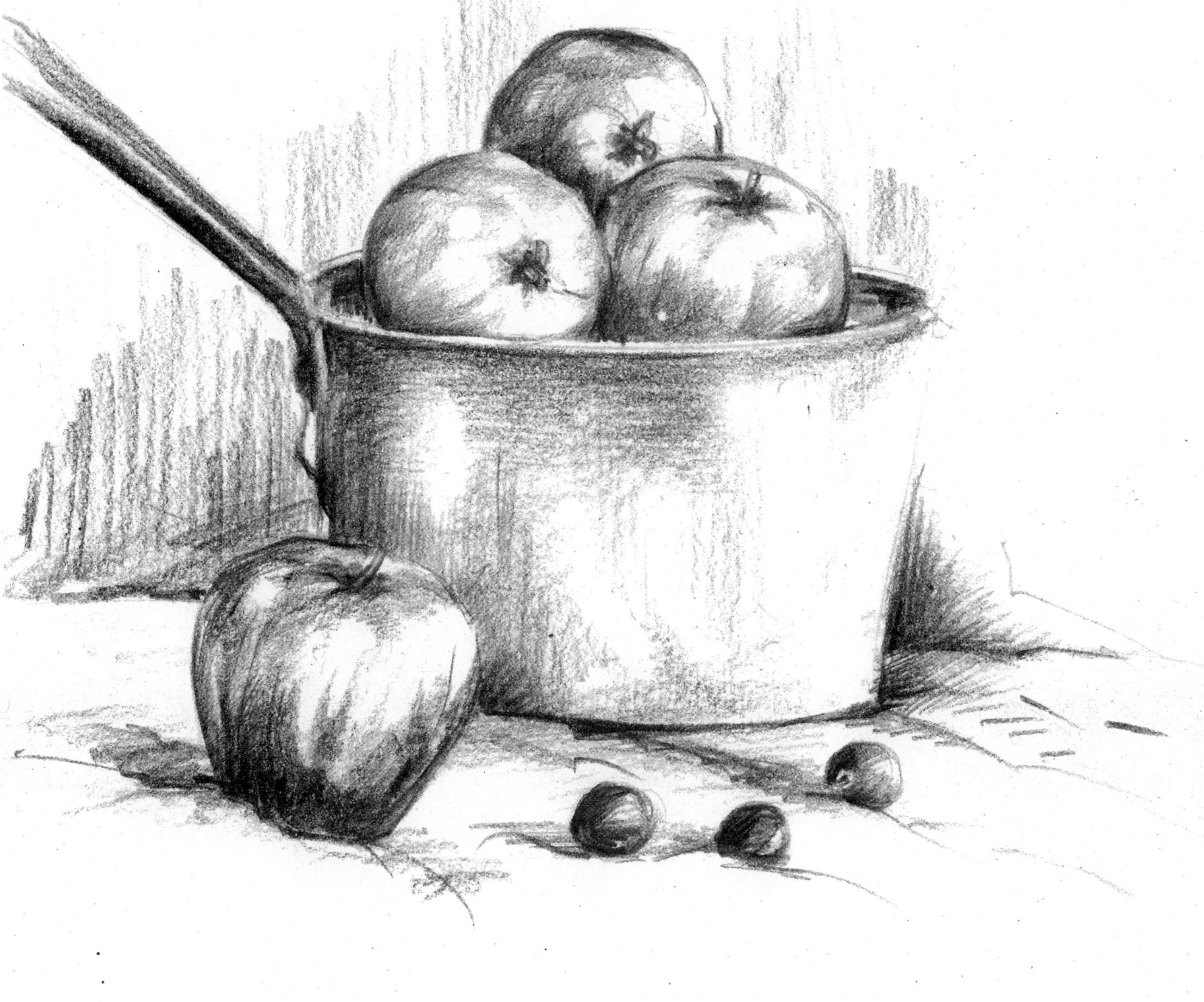

Keep coming back to the basics whenever you choose a new subject to draw. On all these pages I have tried several angles and poses to study the form. Have a close look on them and copy if you like.

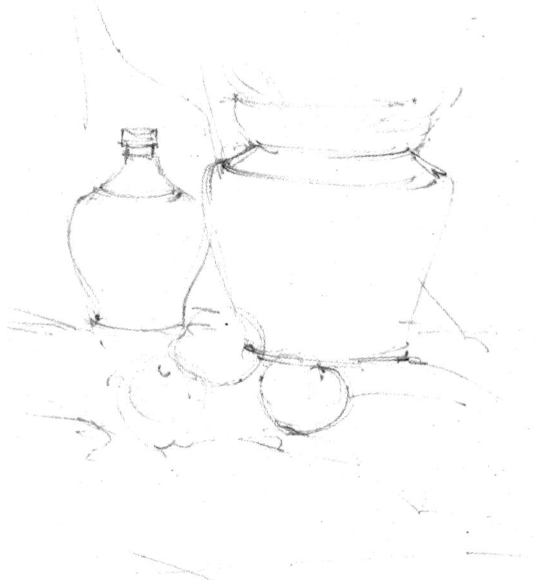

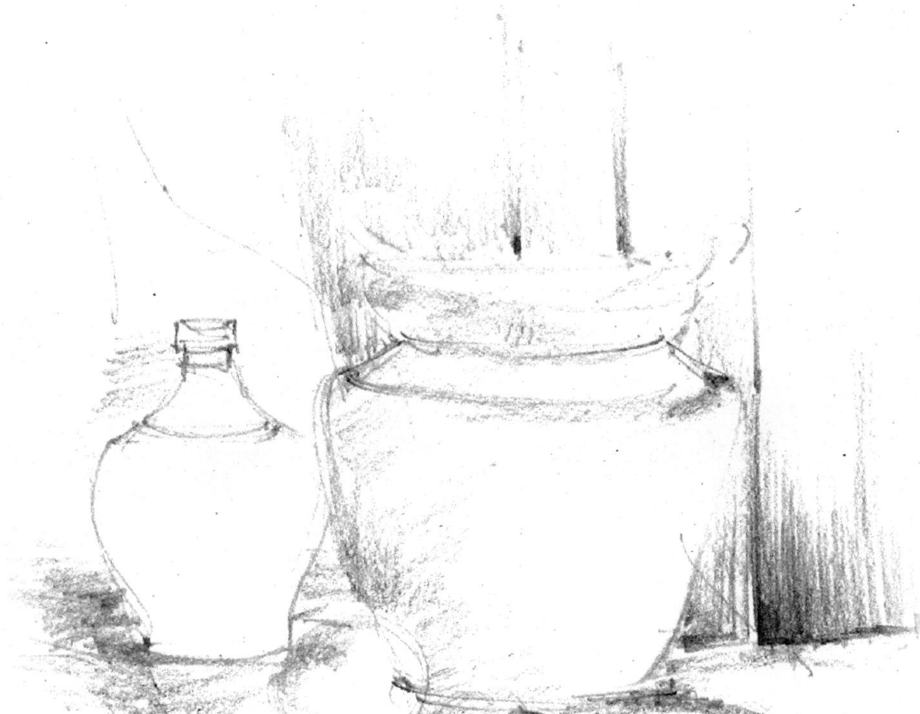

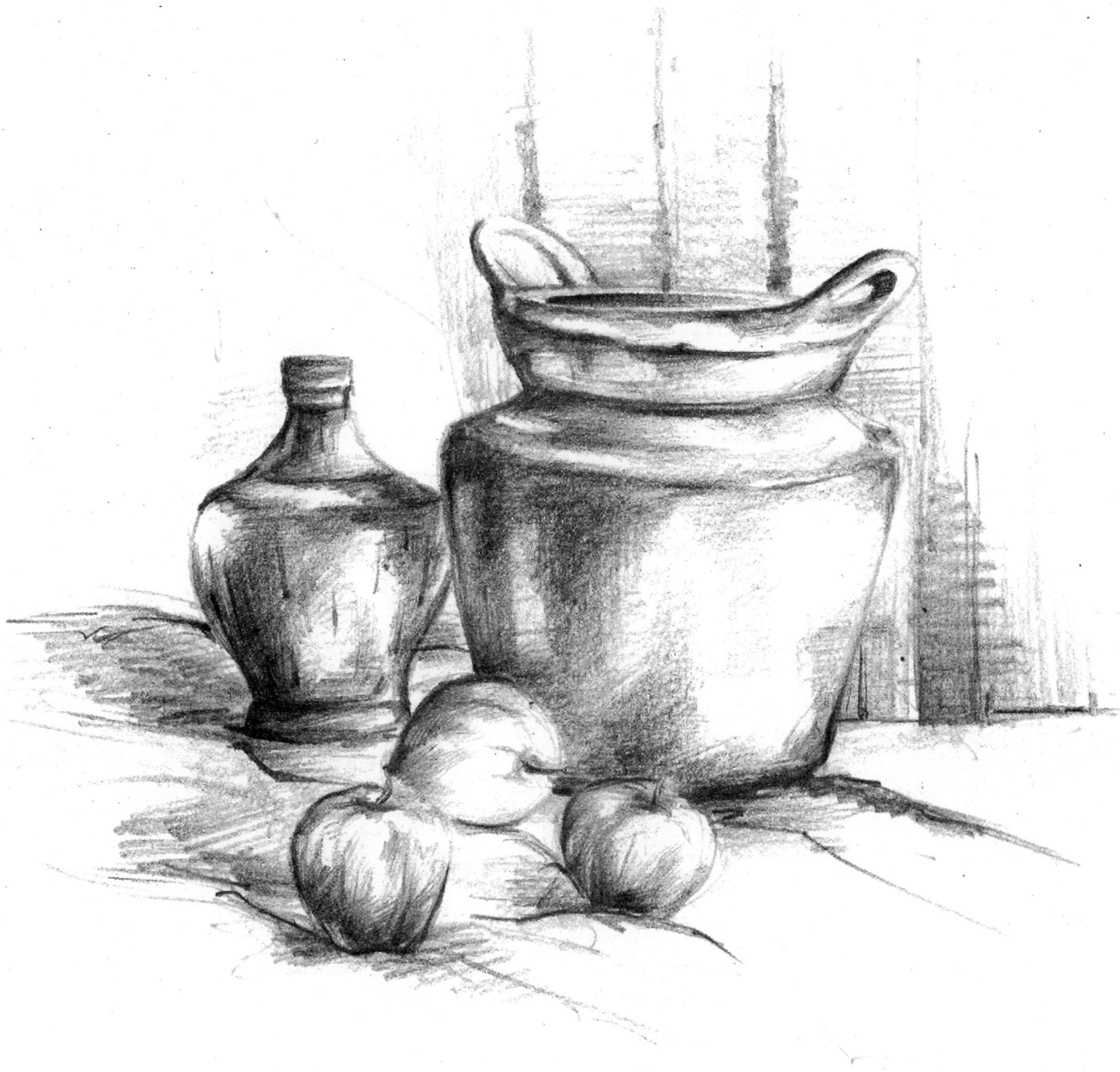

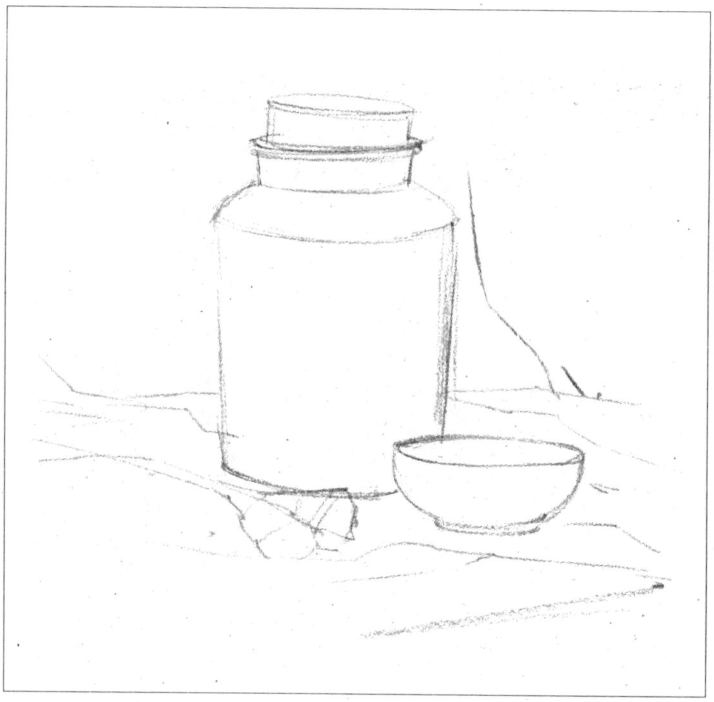

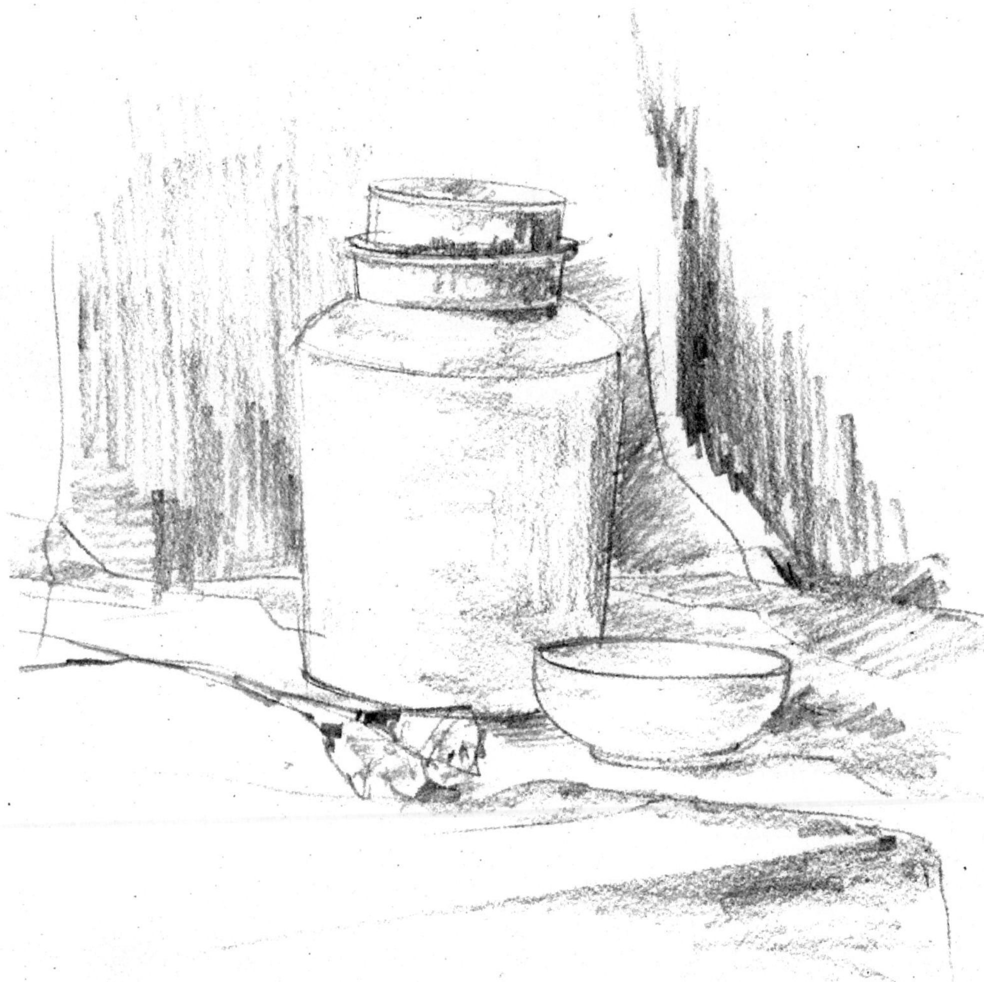

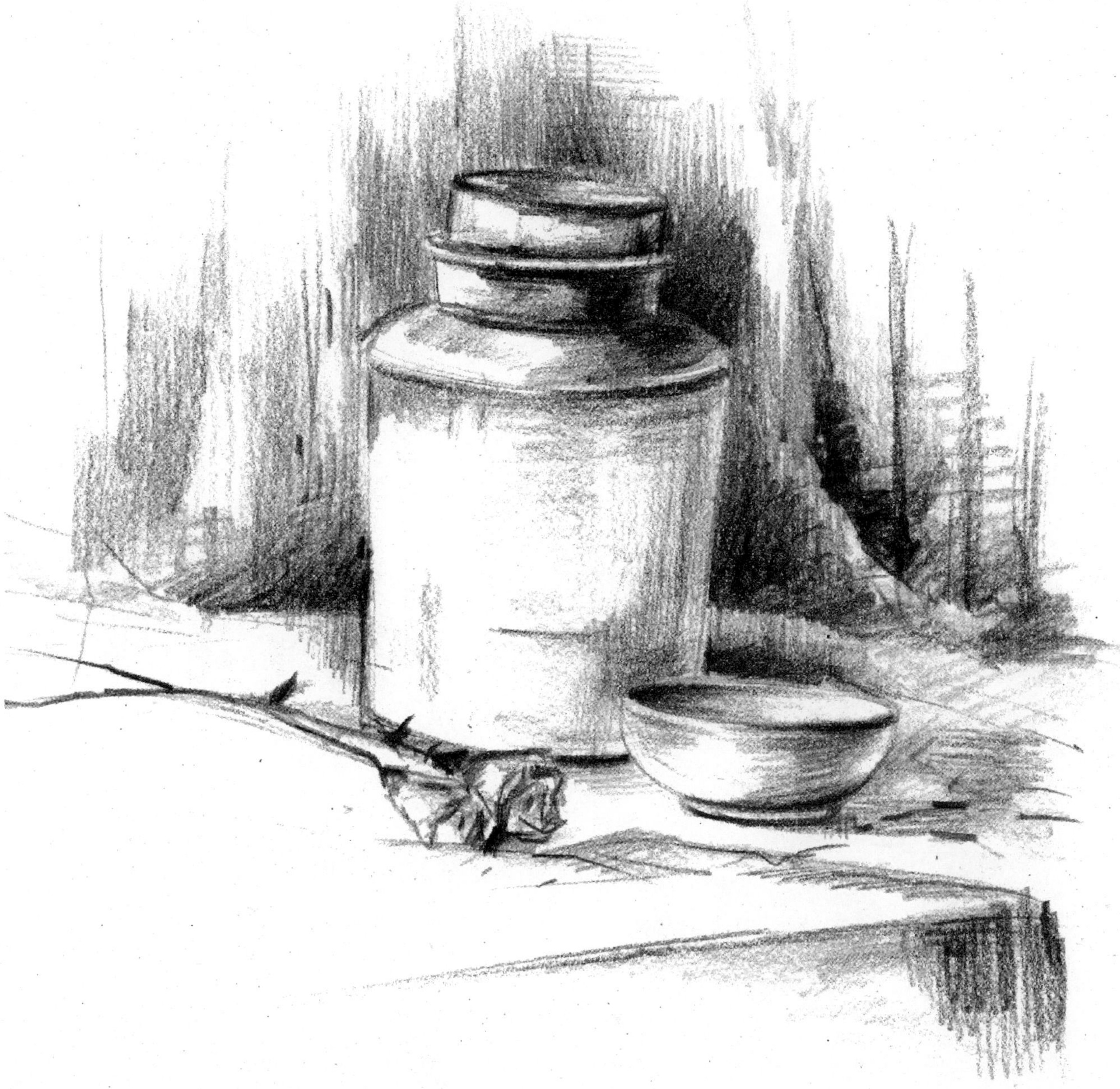

In nature, practically everything is a good subject for drawing. So draw what you like. Remember, line drawing is always important because it provides the structure, shades only create volume and planes. Another factor which become significant here is the way you define texture.

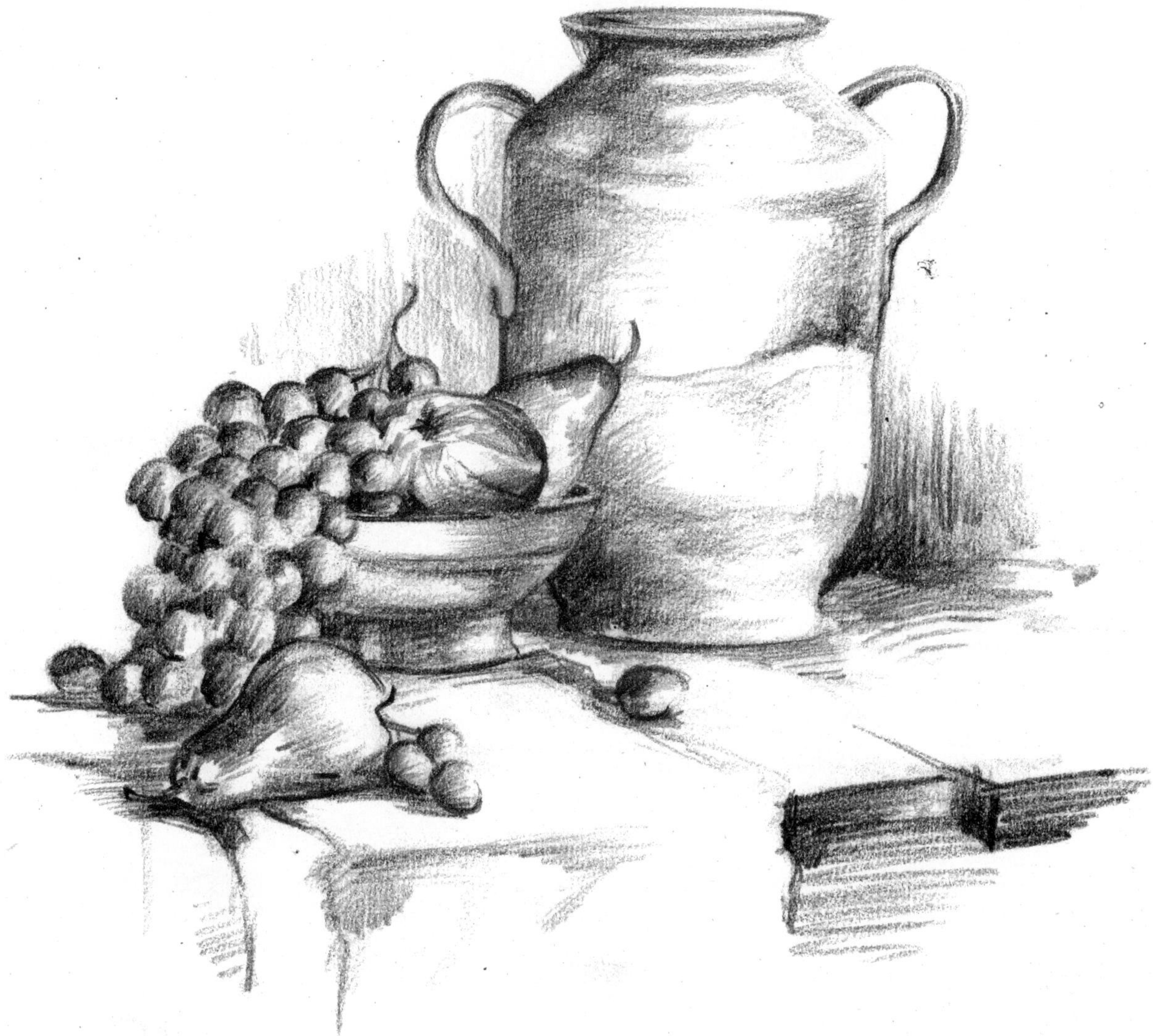

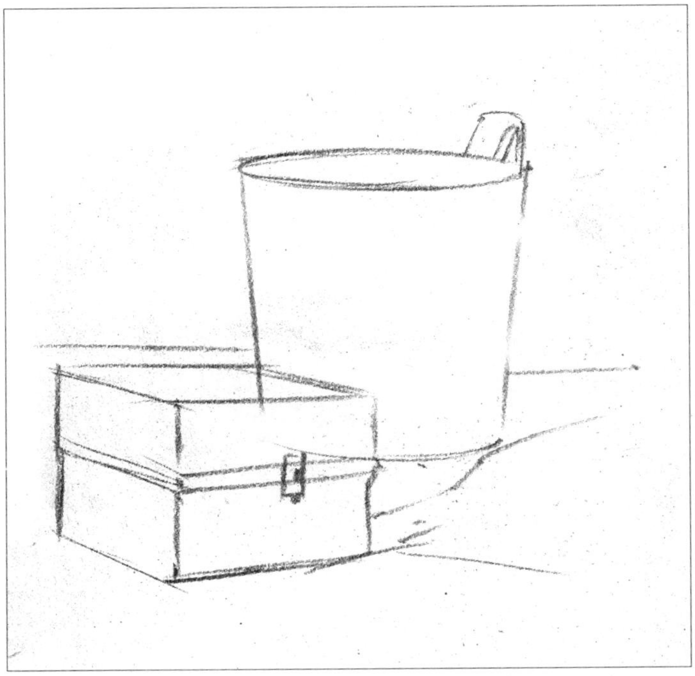

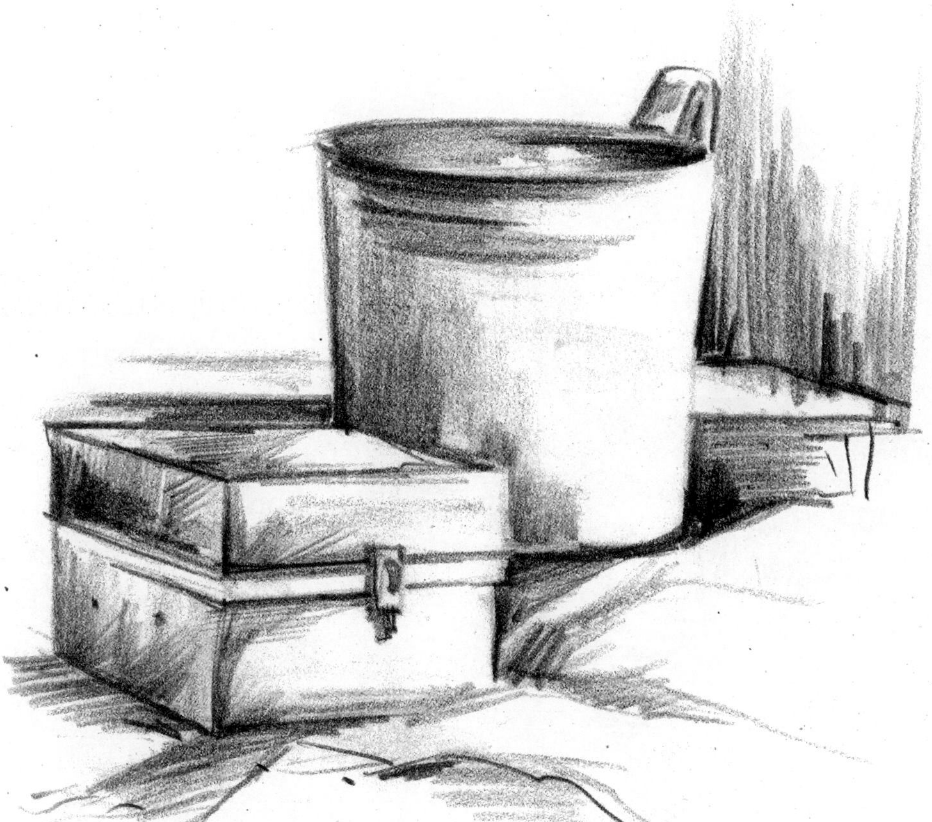

Drapery

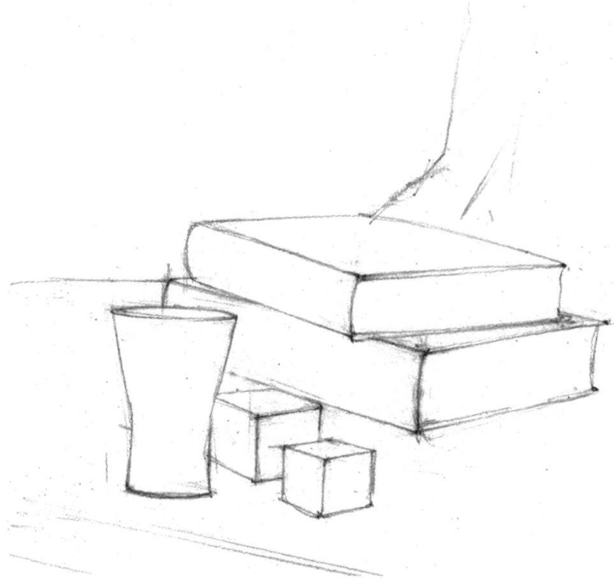

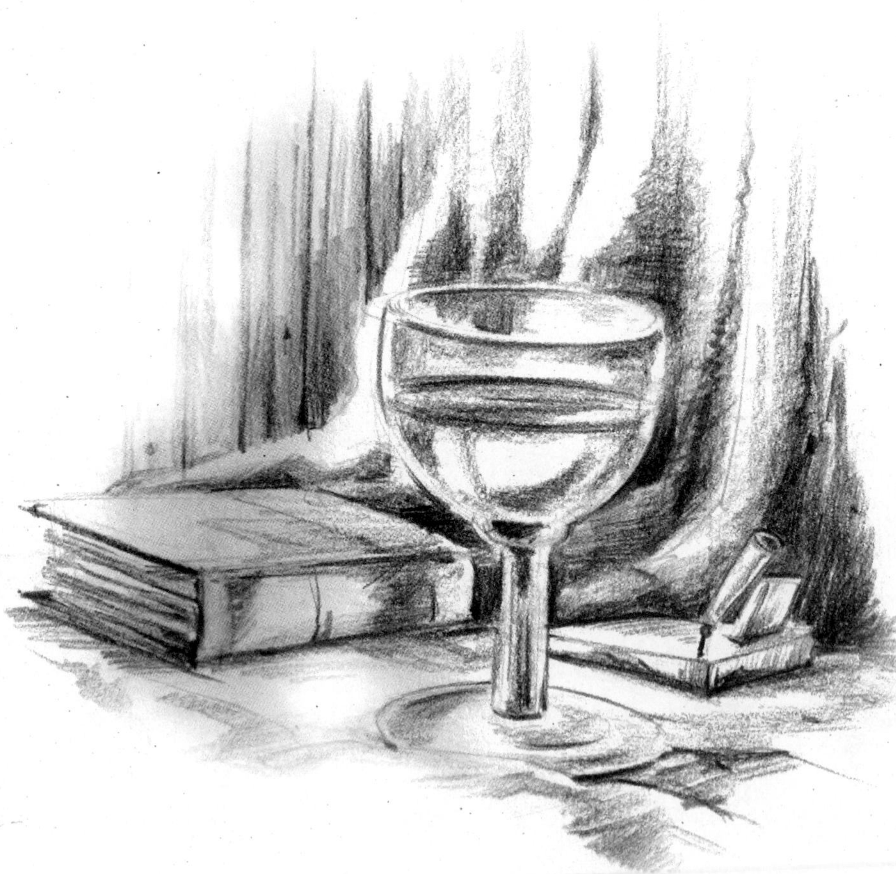

To study still life we mostly use drapery, as drapery brings out the foreground subject. You should learn to give strokes to drapery. In the first step we need to use thin line to get the drapery, and then in the second step we define the highlighted part as well the middle tone. In the third step in the dark area of the drapery, we always should give pencil strokes. If you follow this picture and study it properly you will be able to grasp the exact way to draw drapery.

How to Colour

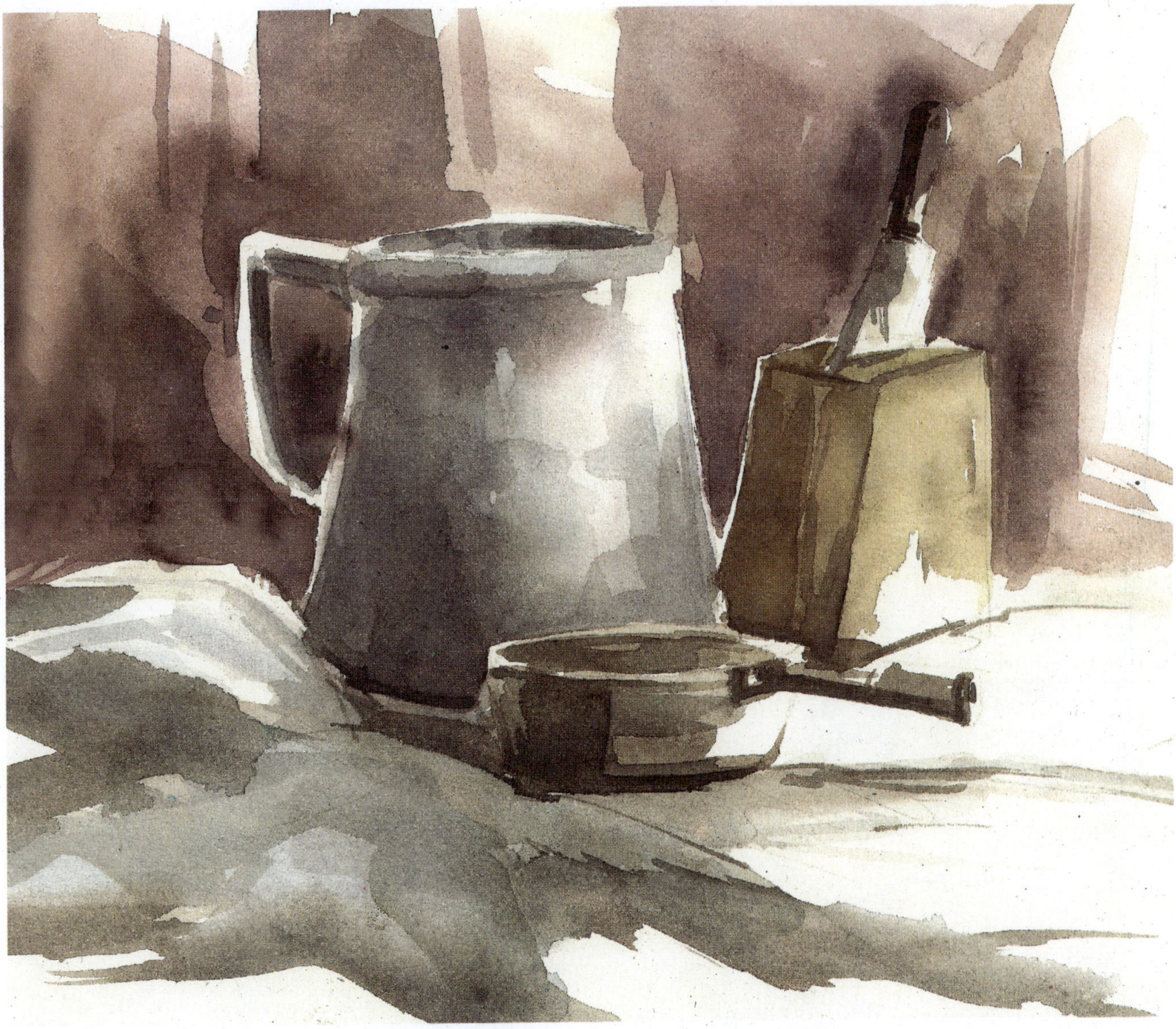

To get the exact colour of still life, pastel colour plays a vital role. Basically we can use paper colour as a middle tone and can start colouring the picture. Making the source of light as the centre, we can bring out the dark part of the subject. But side by side, we should keep in mind that in some cases paper white might come to use, their first tone, second tone and third tone is given by direct use of colour. This picture is an example.

Drapery and Wooden Structure

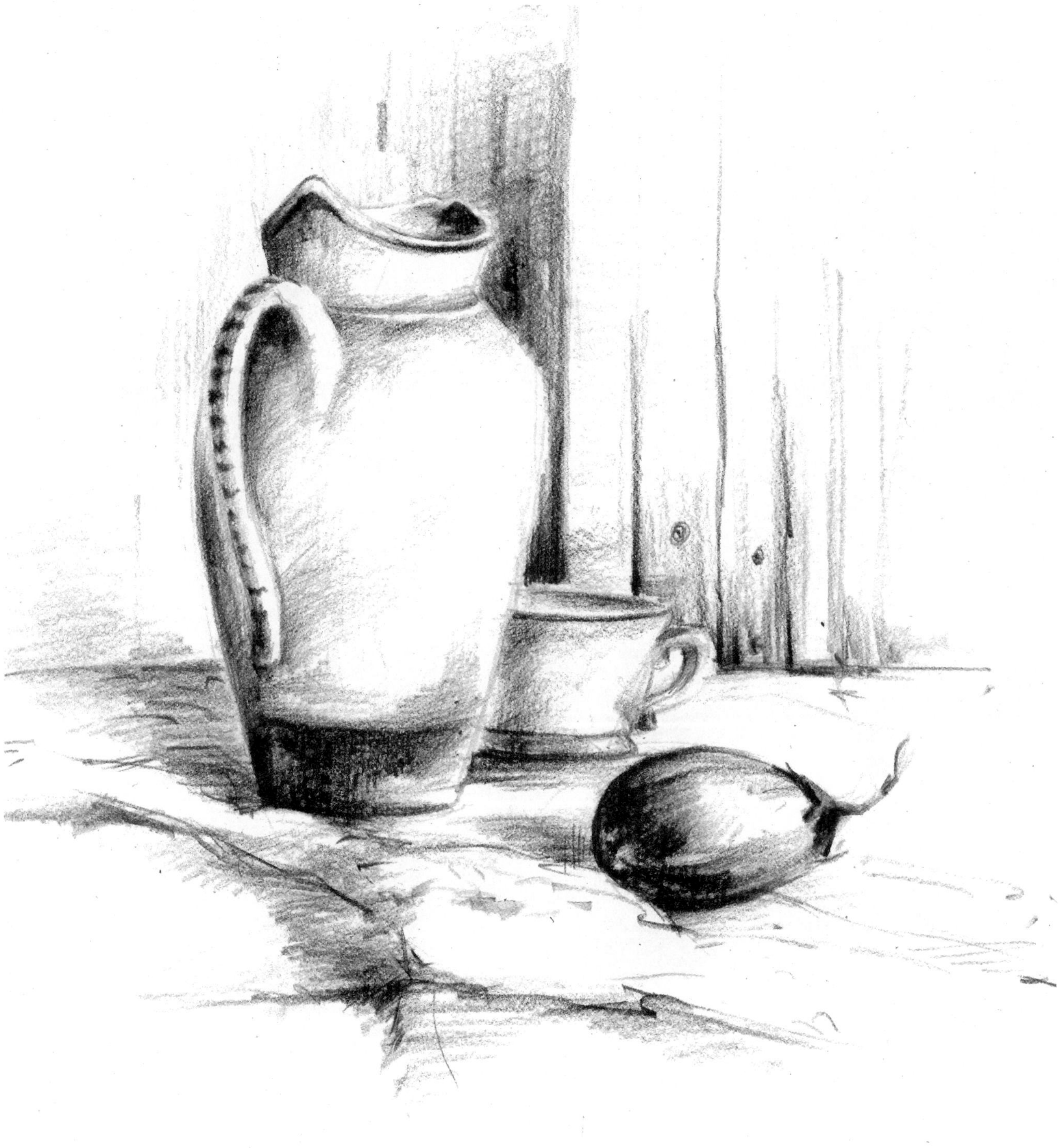

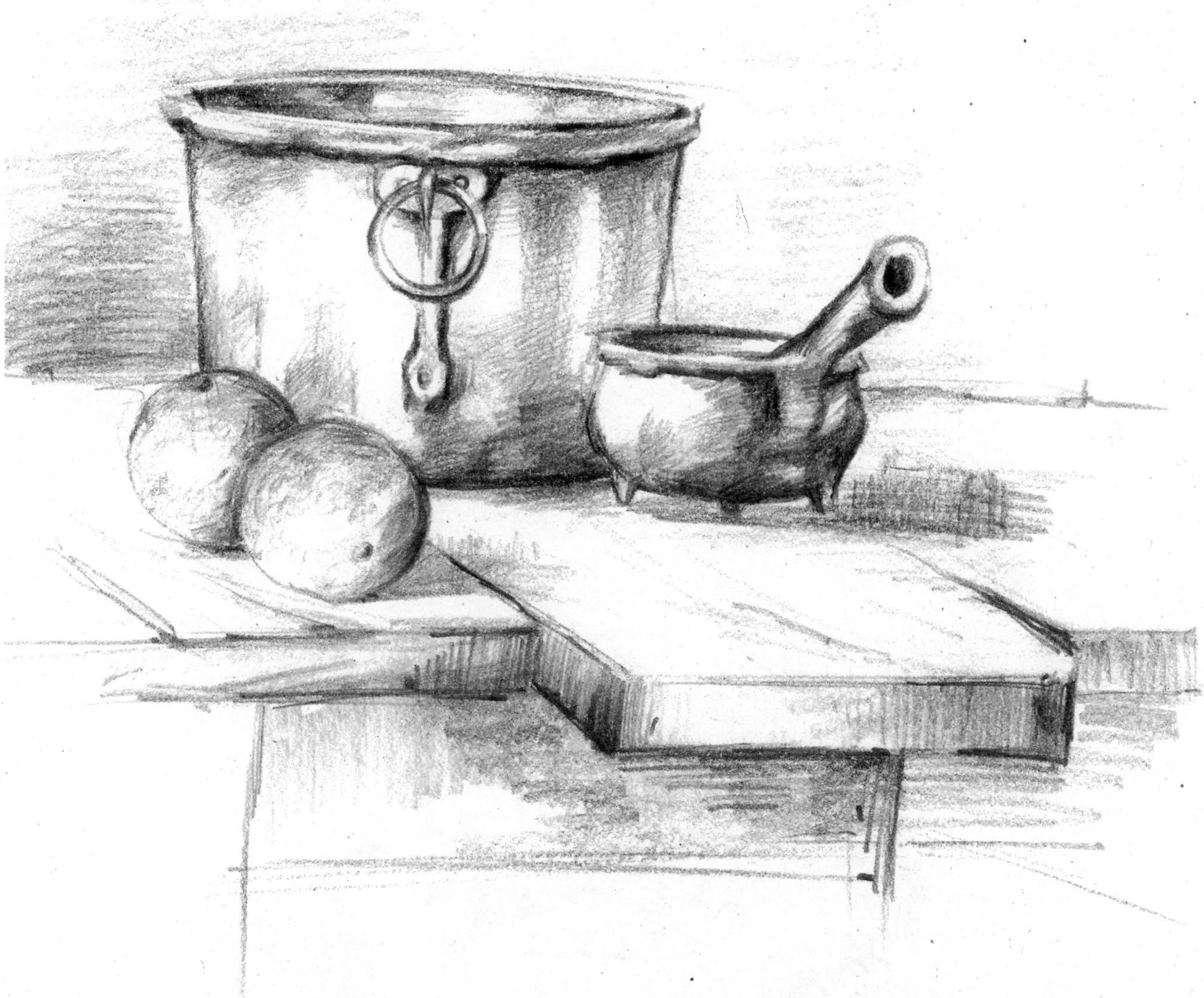

In this picture you will be given proper details about pencil strokes. The interesting part of still life study is that we can study various kinds of materials properly. We will learn how to give pencil strokes to a wooden structure and to a drapery. As both the materials are very different the character of their strokes will also be different. We should first decide what kind of pencil strokes should be given and which are appropriate for texture and for drapery. Then step-by-step we should give light tone, middle tone and dark tone to bring out the exact character of the subject.

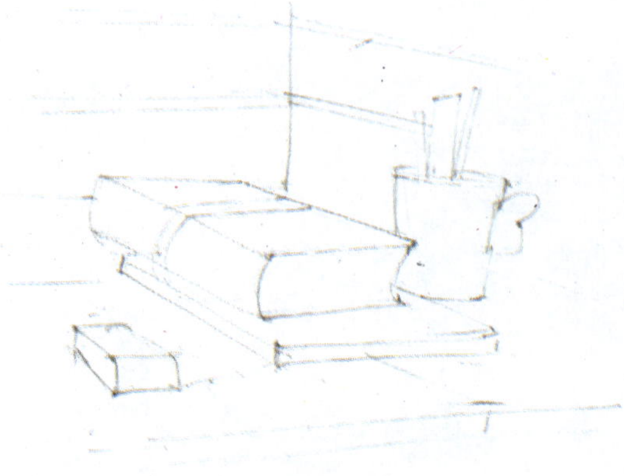

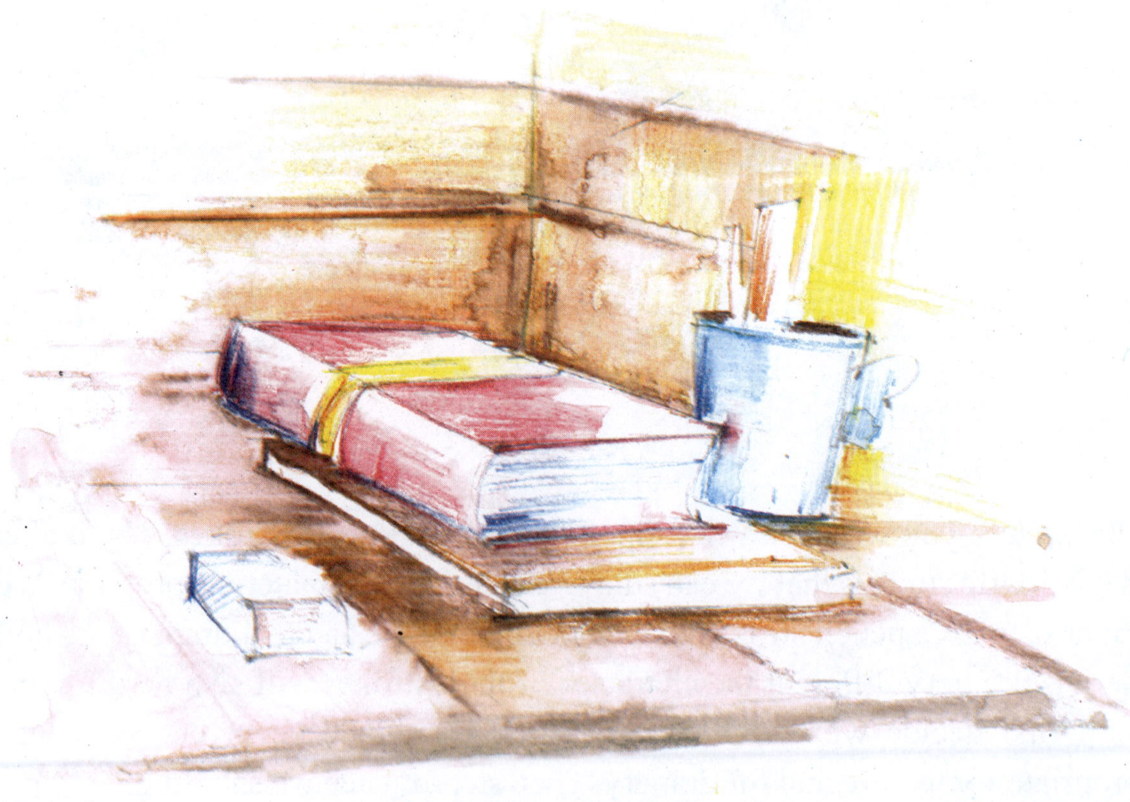

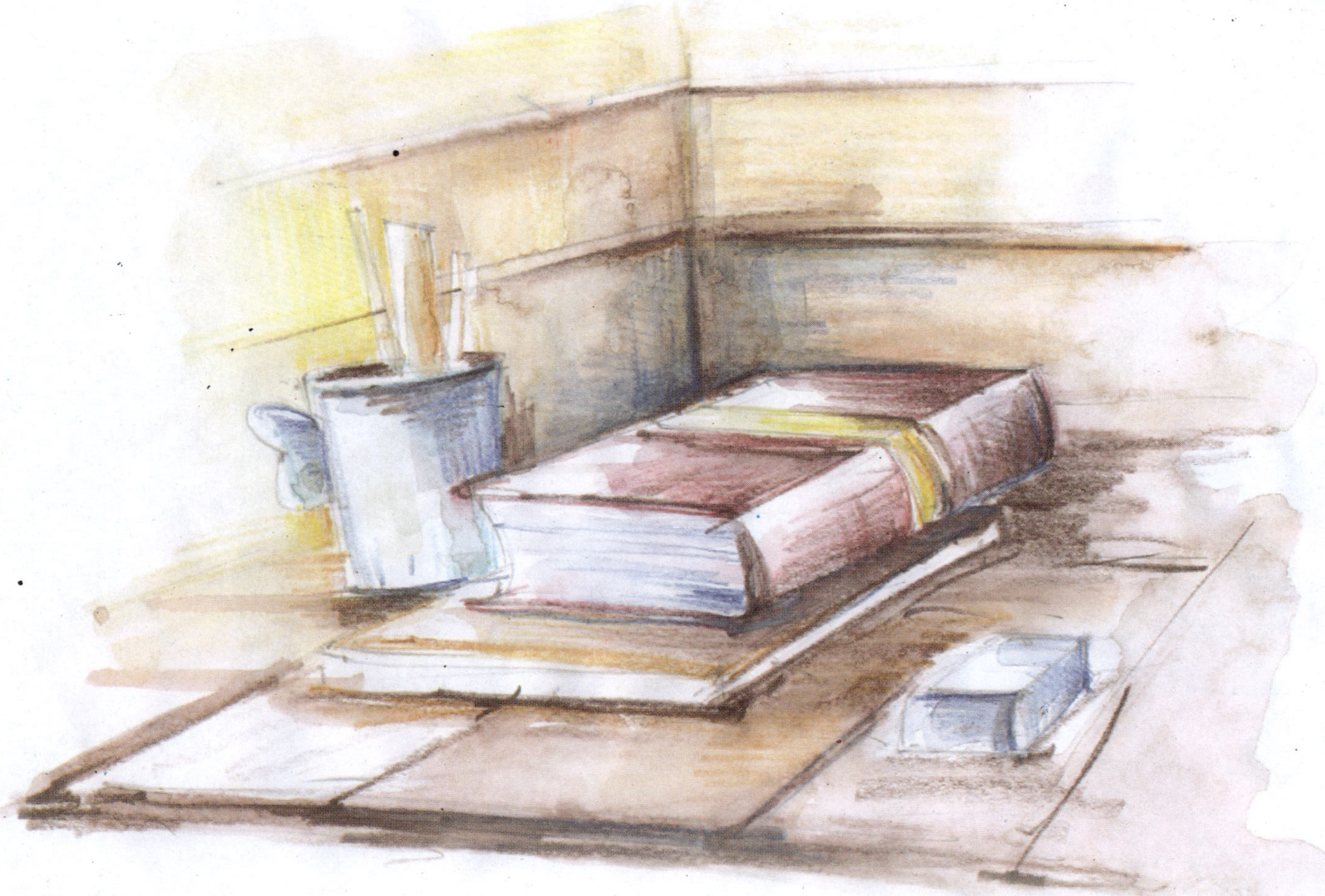

To learn multicolour in still life, monochrome colour is the basic step, as in monochrome colour study we can bring out the highlight, middle tone and depth by using just one colour and using paper white.

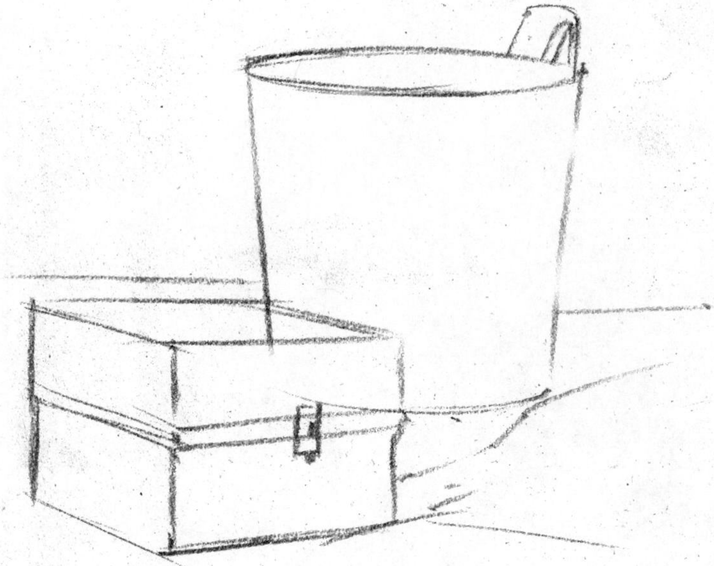

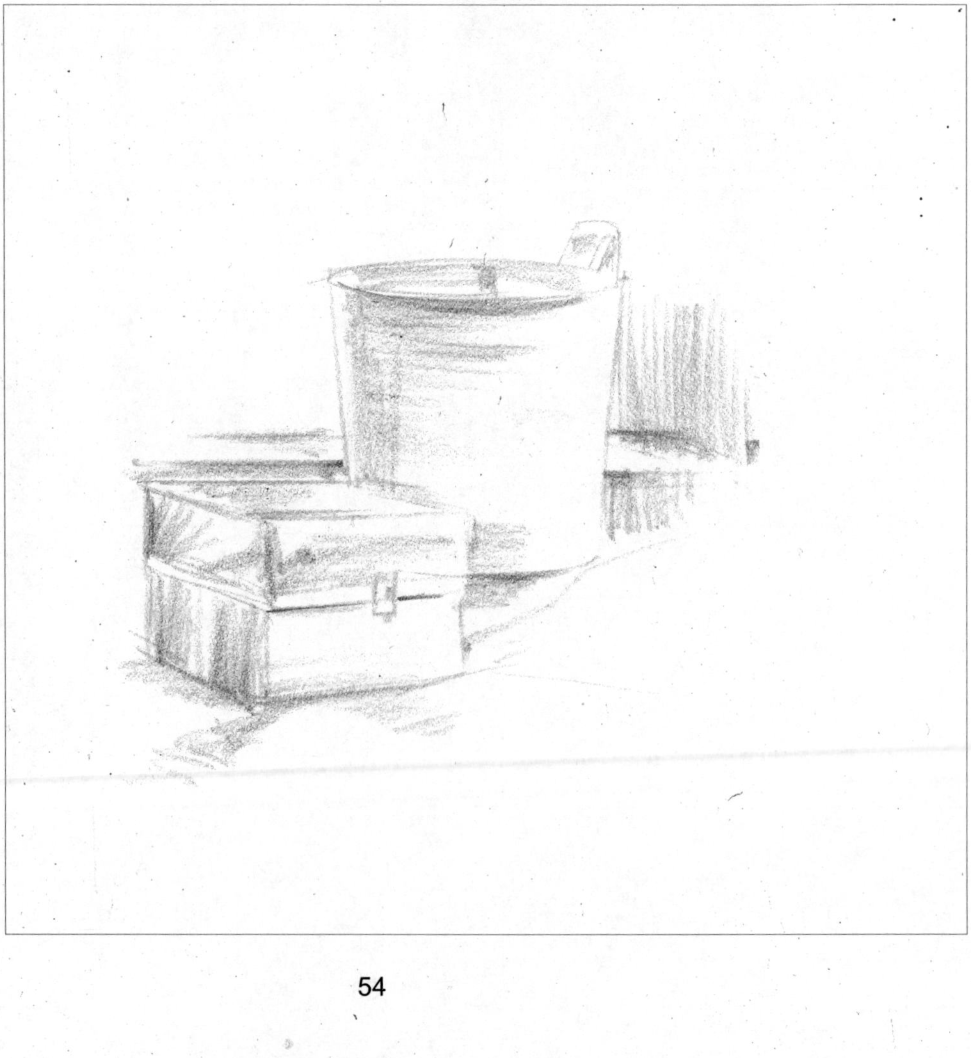

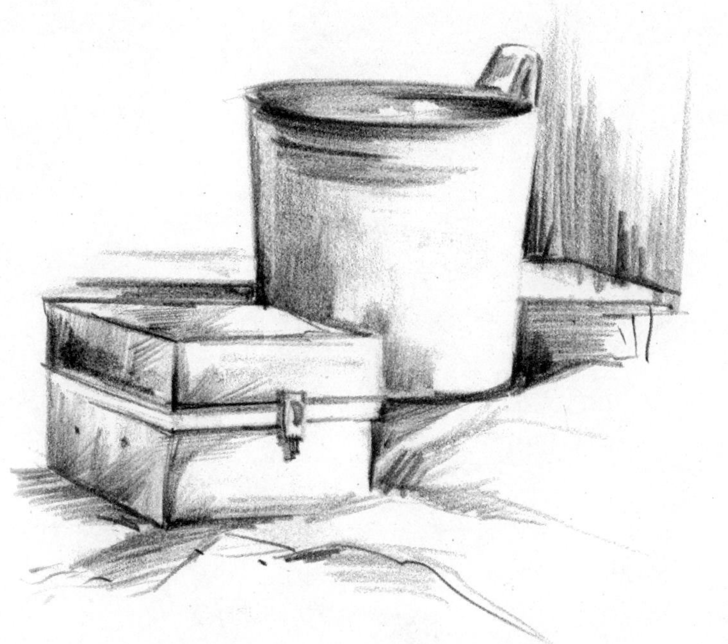

If you have selected a photograph to draw, then remember that you will have to create the perspective by diffusing things which are placed further and away from you.

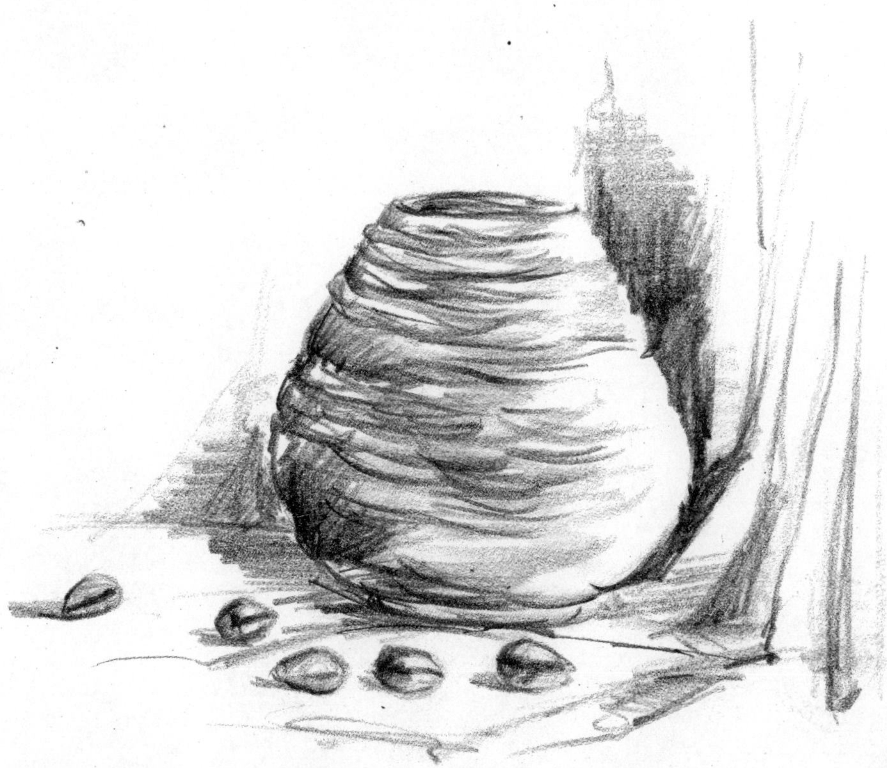

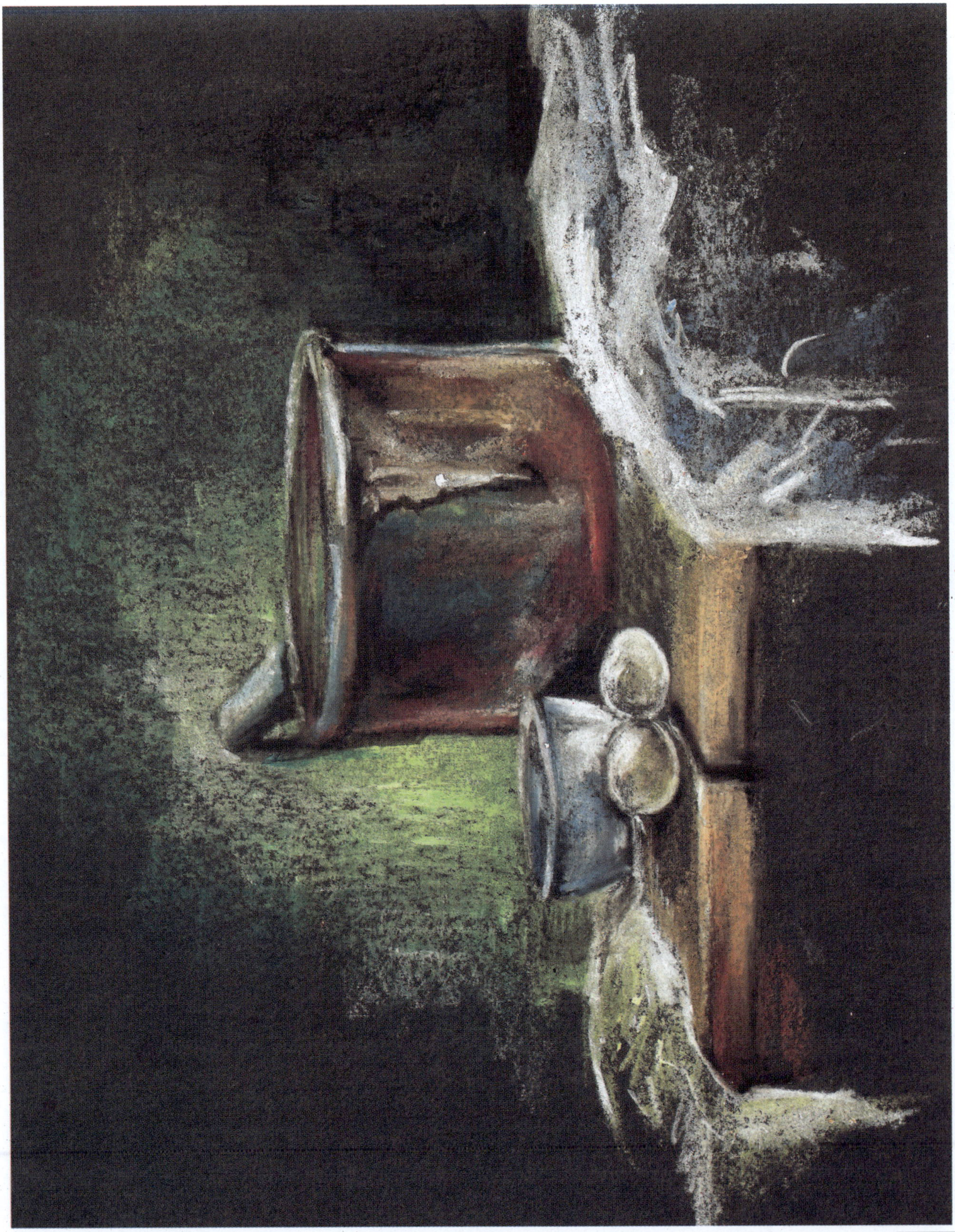

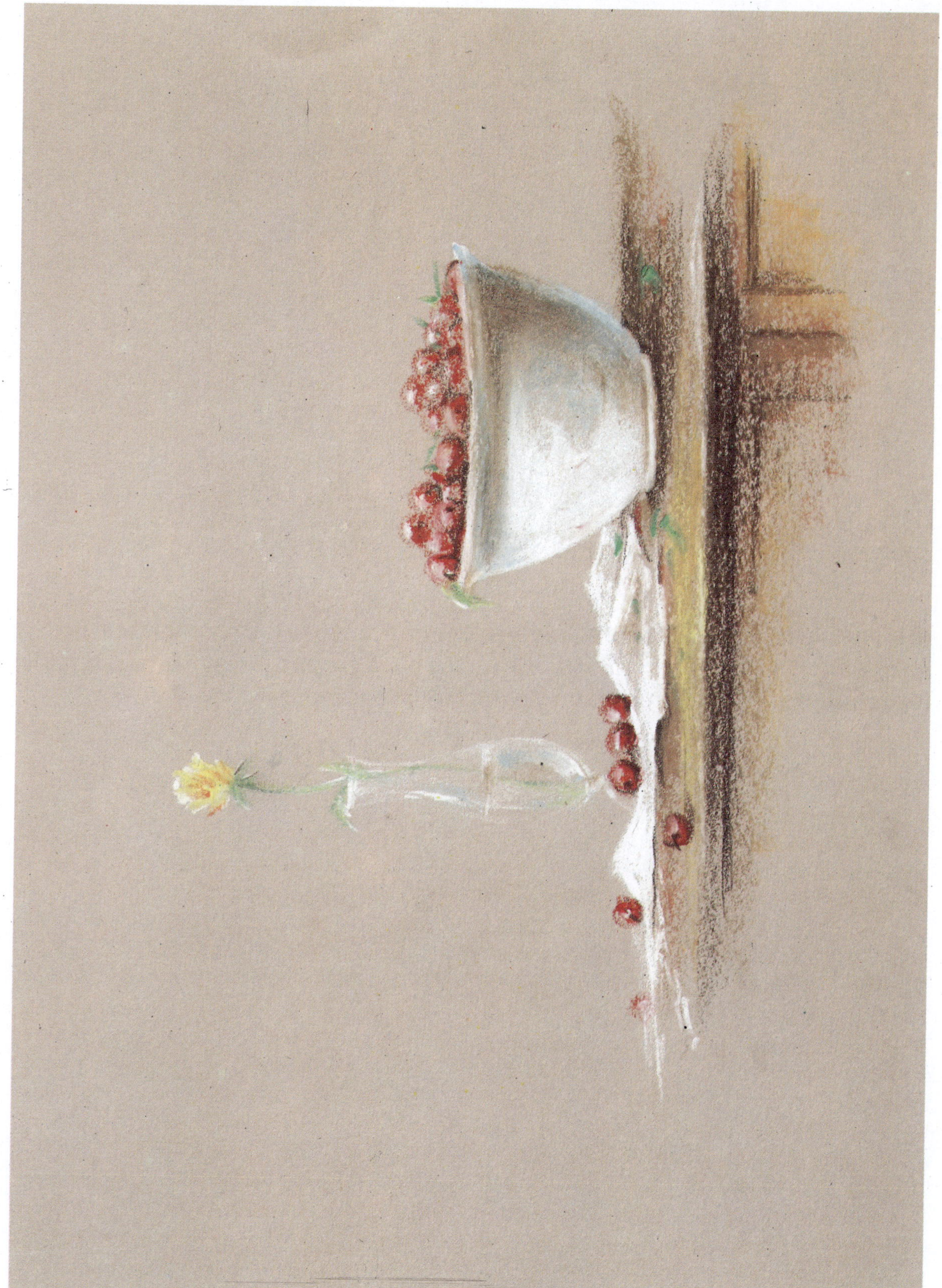

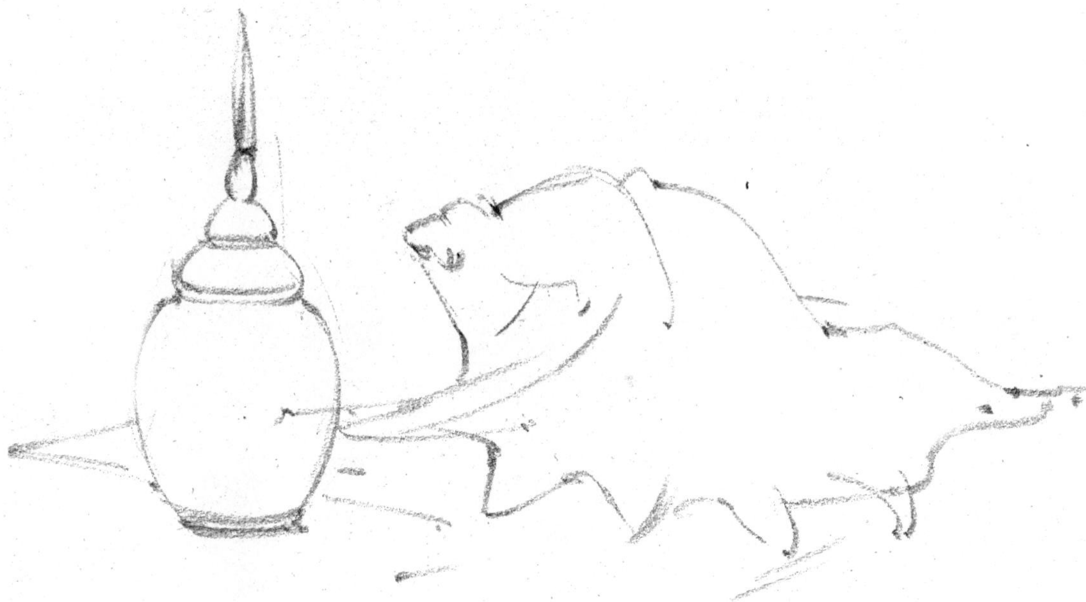

In many cases of still life we always give importance to the character on the foreground, as the subject of still life on the background always brings out the foreground properly. This picture is one of the examples.

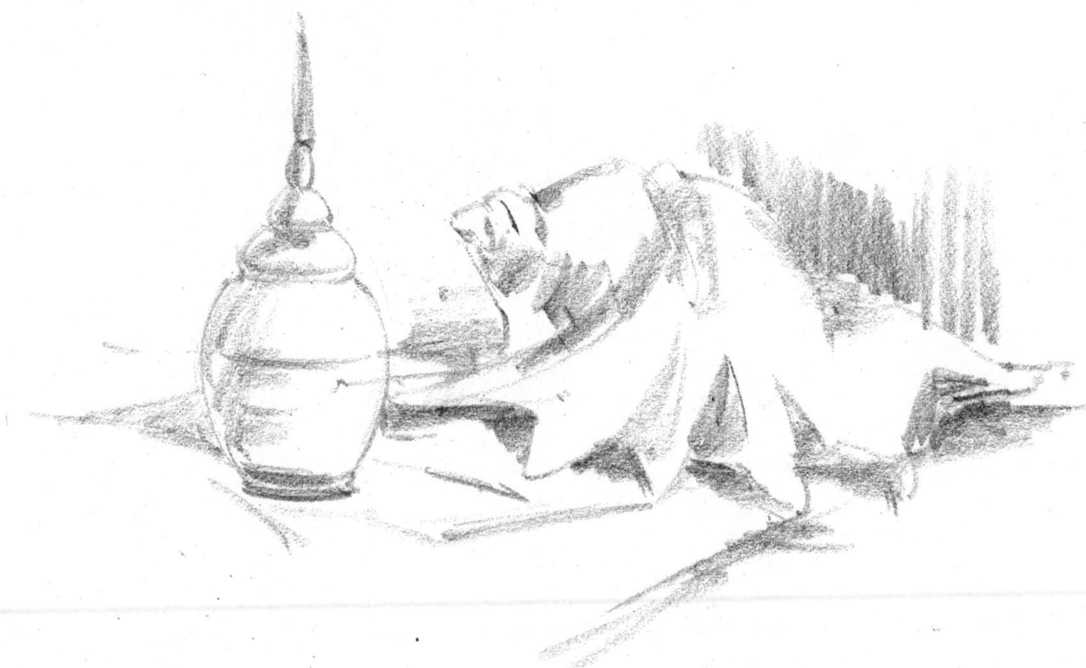

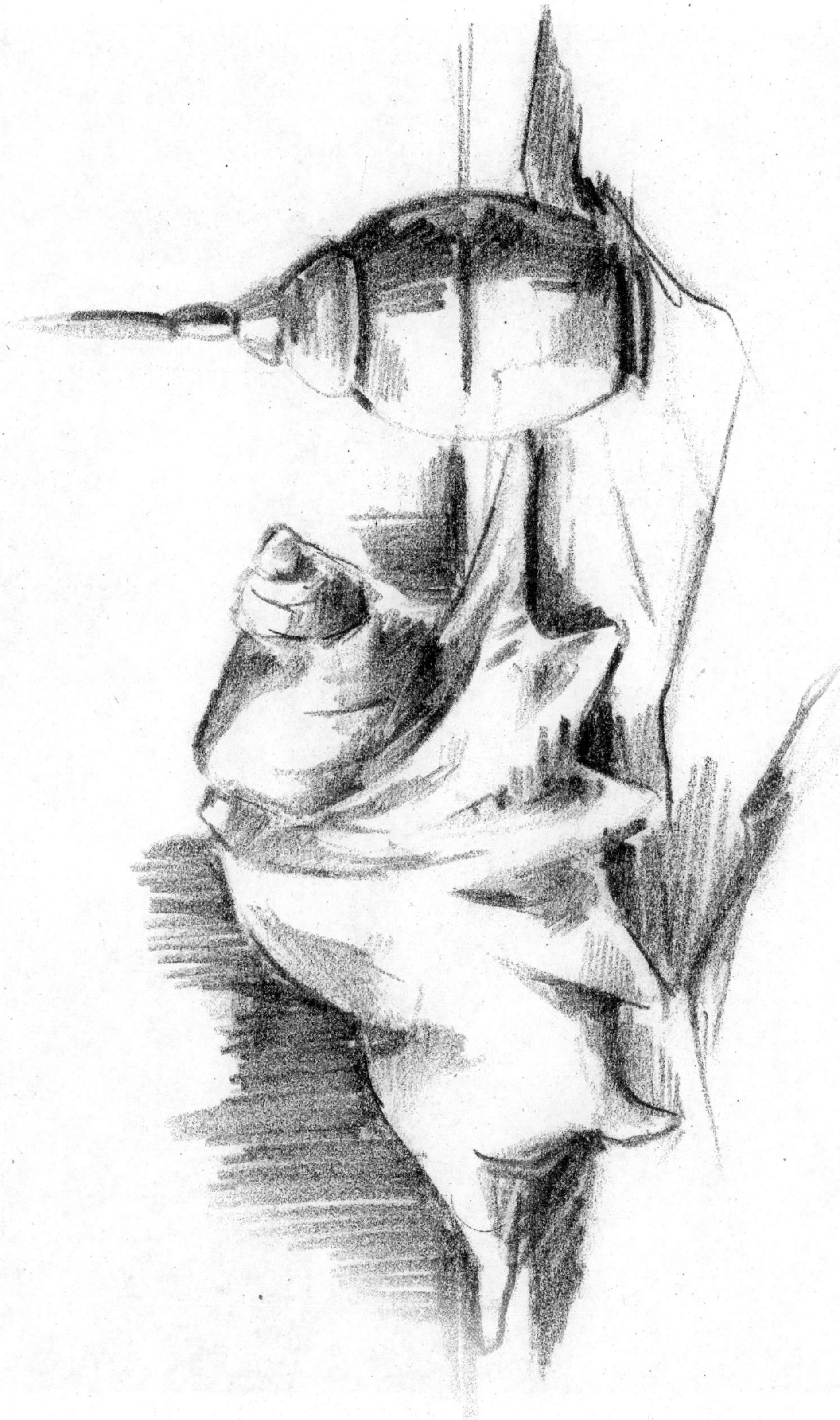

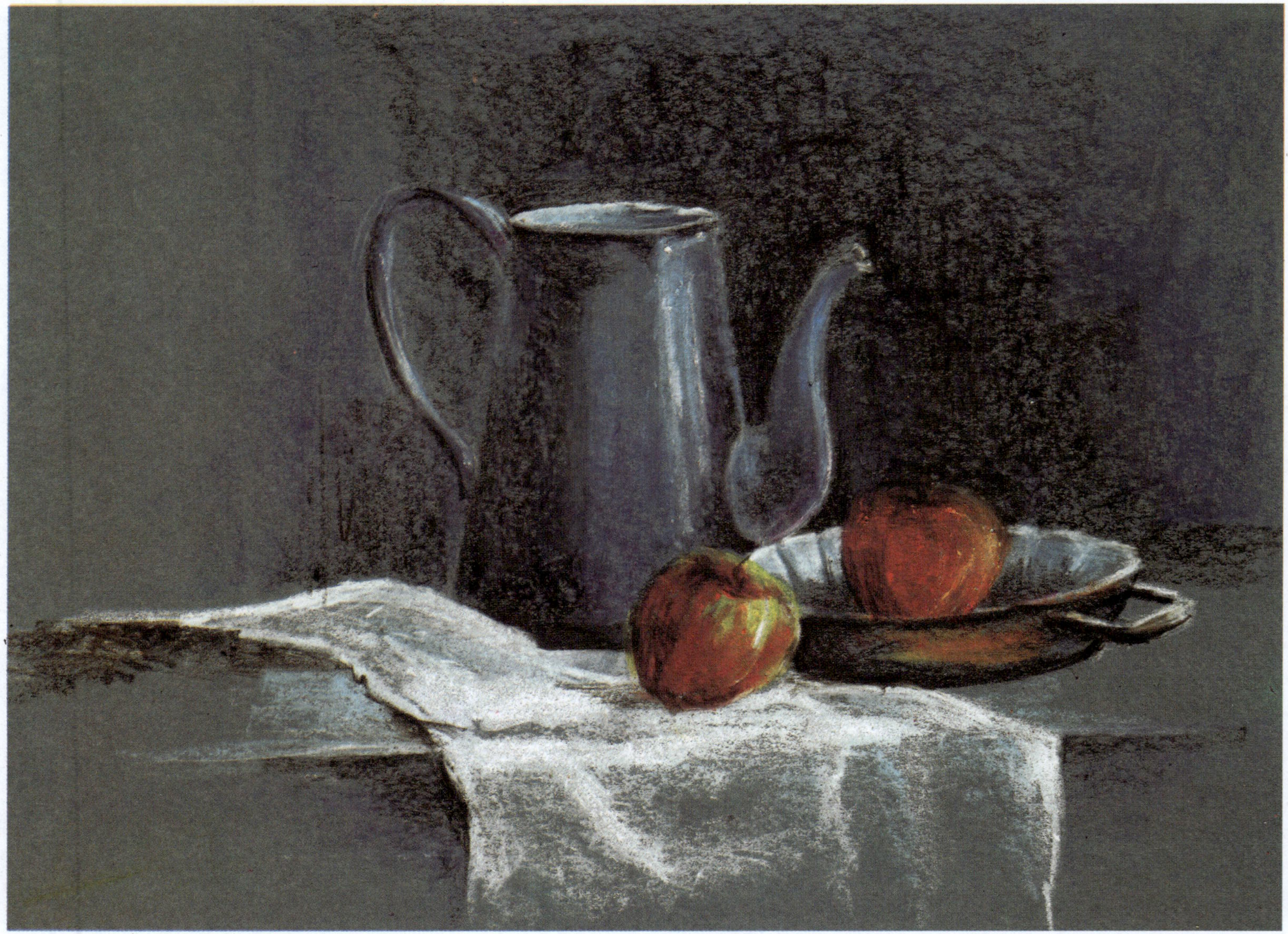

Practice makes a man perfect, so does hard work. So best of luck, while you keep embarking on new journeys and achieve different goals and targets. Keep drawing and practising new techniques.

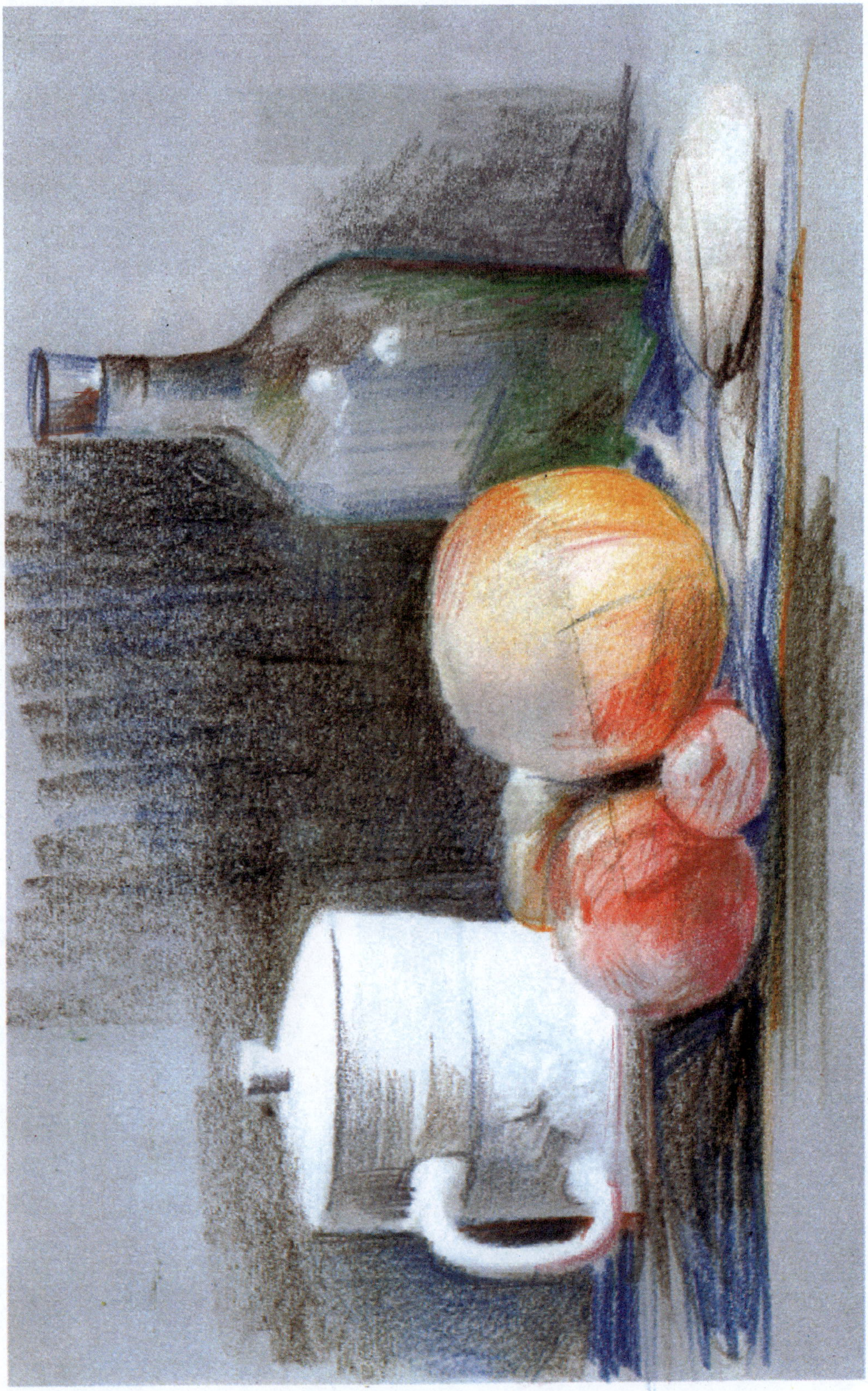

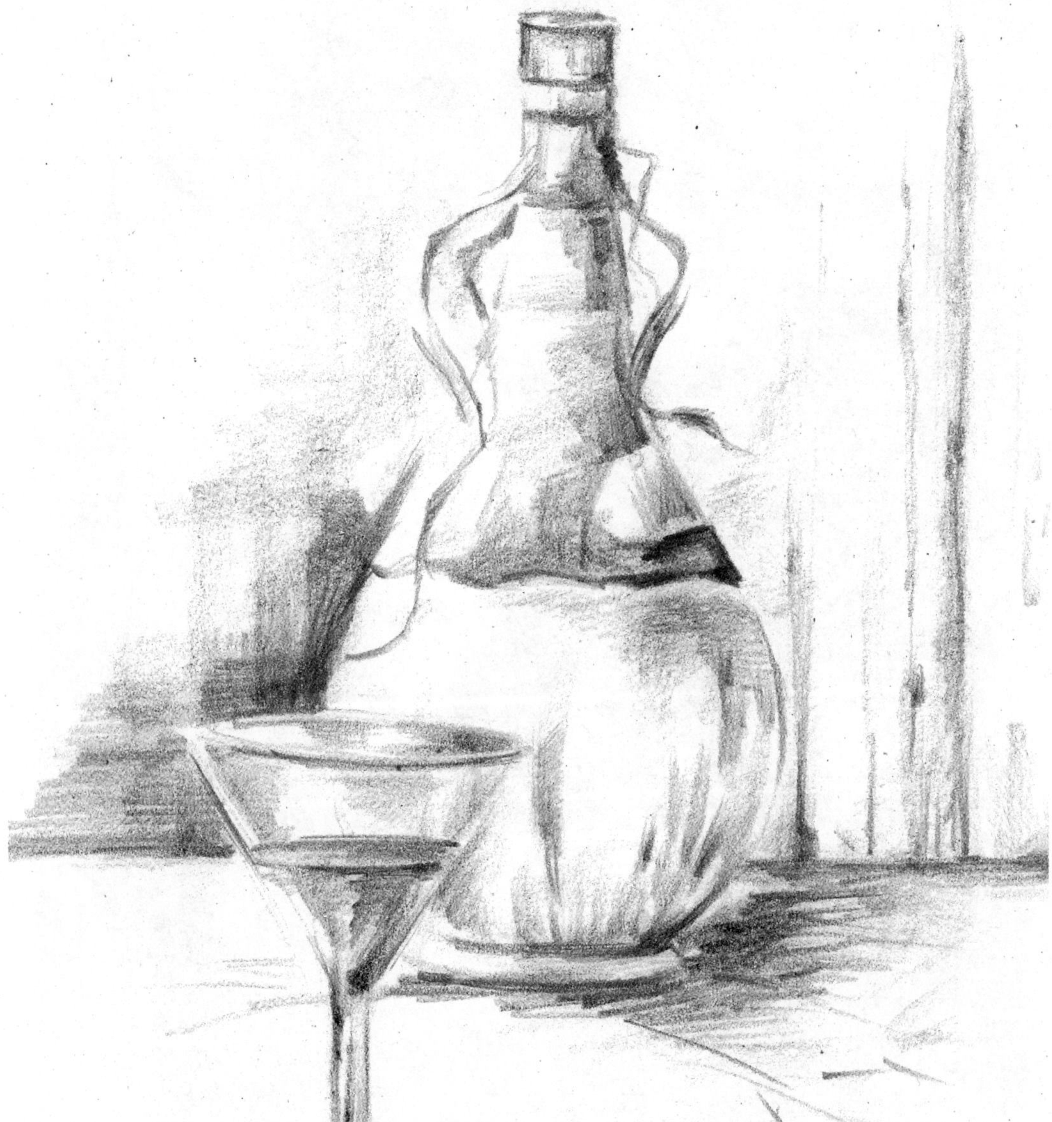

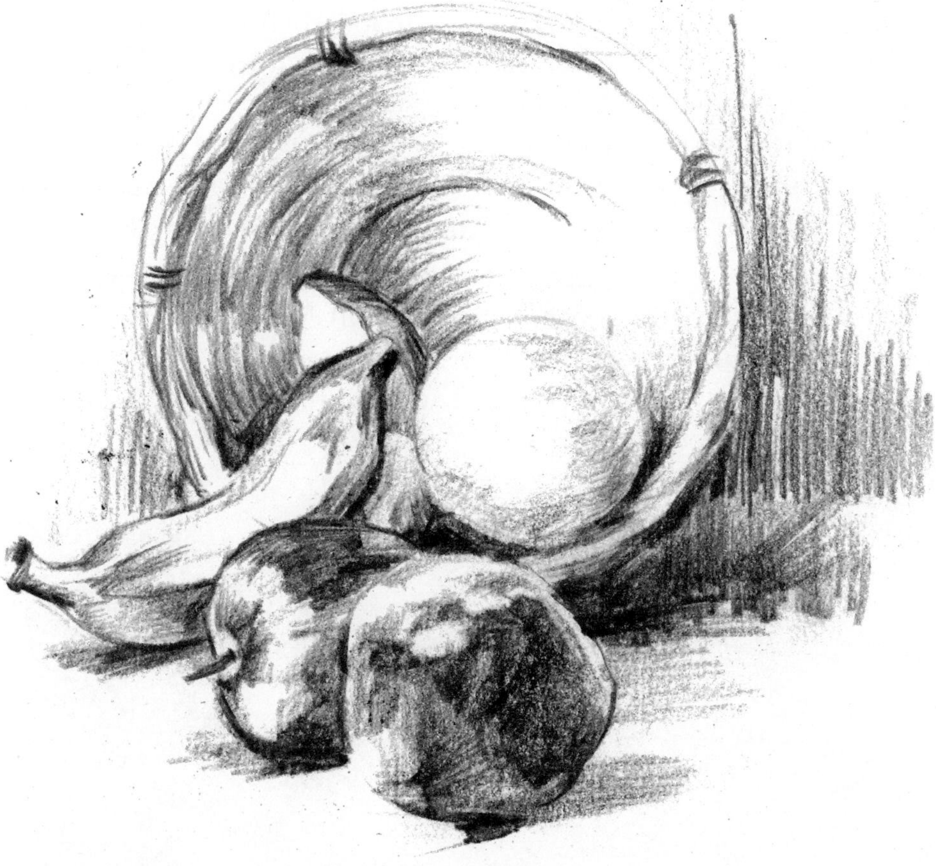

A fine line drawing contain the whole statement of whatever you want to express, so keep things simple but accurate.

You should be able to recognize the basic and structural forms in a certain pose. The larger and smaller areas may differ in size but the identical volume and form will always be there.

Always draw in a natural way which is most suitable to you. If you want to add lot of detail, do it. If you like to work in a few defining lines, it is good. Here natural way means what is natural to you, which suits you well. Keep things simple. Simplicity is the ultimate attainment of art and beginning of nature and when drawing becomes natural to you, than time and you will become your own teacher. So be a child. Take things as they come in your life and keep drawing every thing you like.

Whoever can hold a pencil can draw or sketch. The problem arises only when you start comparing your drawing with those of the others and add some definition to it. We ourselves are the main obstacle in our progress as an artist and the cause lines with false conceptions. How about your childhood when things were not so tough for you.? When drawing a complex landscape consisting of mountains, trees, rivers and, of course, a small hut was so easy. It was so, because then we were used to expressing things in a very simple way. What we lost today is the great confidence we had.

Every artist starts with the three triangles representing mountains circle as sun and two curved, unbalanced lines as river. This very person when some day will draw your portrait, you seem to transfer on paper with life sparking in your eyes. This Mr. X can be you, if "you" think it is worth try. The positive thoughts and daily diddling with pencil will do the rest.

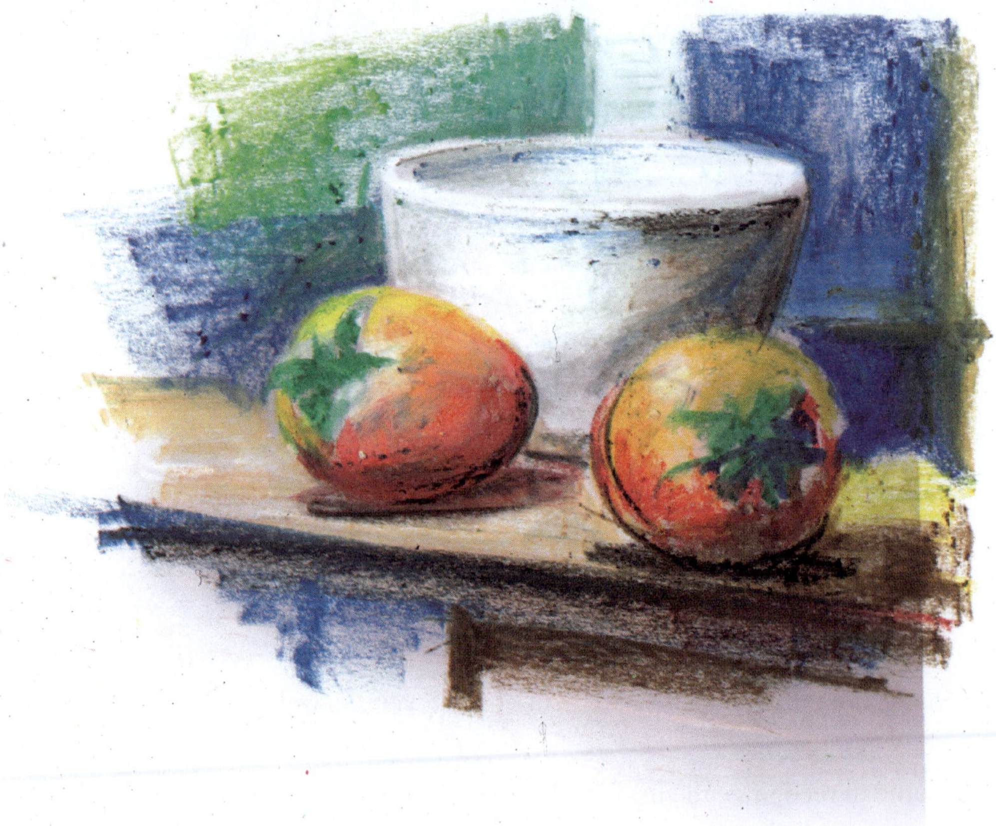